SEX AND SEXUALITY IN
VICTORIAN
BRITAIN

This book is dedicated to:
Hannah Cullwick, a woman who knew what she wanted
(and what she didn't); Elizabeth 'Lizzie' Siddal, who deserved better;
Evelina Marmon, who did her best and was betrayed; and Emma
Jones, one of many, but never forgotten.

SEX AND SEXUALITY IN
VICTORIAN
BRITAIN

VIOLET FENN

PEN & SWORD **HISTORY**

AN IMPRINT OF PEN & SWORD BOOKS LTD.
YORKSHIRE - PHILADELPHIA

First published in Great Britain in 2020 by
PEN AND SWORD HISTORY
An imprint of
Pen & Sword Books Ltd
Yorkshire – Philadelphia

ISBN 978 1 52675 668 8

A CIP catalogue record for this book is available from the British Library.

Typeset in Times New Roman 11.5/14 by
Aura Technology and Software Services, India.
Printed and bound in the UK by TJ International.

Pen & Sword Books Limited incorporates the imprints of Atlas, Archaeology,
Aviation, Discovery, Family History, Fiction, History, Maritime, Military, Military
Classics, Politics, Select, Transport, True Crime, Air World, Frontline Publishing,
Leo Cooper, Remember When, Seaforth Publishing, The Praetorian Press,
Wharncliffe Local History, Wharncliffe Transport, Wharncliffe True Crime and
White Owl.

For a complete list of Pen & Sword titles please contact
PEN & SWORD BOOKS LIMITED
47 Church Street, Barnsley, South Yorkshire, S70 2AS, England
E-mail: enquiries@pen-and-sword.co.uk
Website: www.pen-and-sword.co.uk

Or
PEN AND SWORD BOOKS
1950 Lawrence Rd, Havertown, PA 19083, USA
E-mail: Uspen-and-sword@casematepublishers.com
Website: www.penandswordbooks.com

Contents

Introduction..x

Chapter 1   Hustle and Bustle 1

Chapter 2   Beddings, Weddings and Bastards 19

Chapter 3   Liberty, Fraternity, Fidelity 30

Chapter 4   Lifting the Lid on Lust...................................39

Chapter 5   Gentleman's Relish...51

Chapter 6   One Night With Venus, A Lifetime With Mercury..........59

Chapter 7   Dark Desires...68

Chapter 8   A Walk on the Wilde Side 87

Chapter 9   Hidden in Plain Sight....................................100

Postscript..113

Index 116

Acknowledgements

This book wouldn't have made it into existence without the following people. I will invariably have left out at least one essential person. It's absolutely not intentional and if it helps you feel better, I can assure you that I will lie awake cringing about it in the early hours for the rest of my life. I hope you're happy.

Cressida Downing, aka The Book Analyst (thebookanalyst.co.uk), without whom very little of my writing would ever make it out of my head in the first place; The Atkinson museum and art gallery in Southport, particularly Stephen Whittle and Joanne Chamberlain, for allowing me to put their beautiful Lilith on the front cover; Gill Hoffs, who has been an absolute rock and saves my sanity on a regular basis. She writes brilliant books about appalling shipwrecks, you should go buy them all.

Everyone at Highgate Cemetery, particularly Peter Mills, Richard Kuhn, Sarah Tregonning and Nick Powell (let us never forget that 'very difficult' tenth album); the Gladstone family, for kindly inviting me into their home; Karl Davies, Hawarden estate manager; everyone at Gladstone's Library, Hawarden, which is my favourite place on the planet.

Alex Butler, who has been an endless and invaluable source of help and information; Joanne 'Tilly' Melia; Helen Stringer; Yvette Caster; Jim Parkyn; Anthony Rhys (@upsetvictorians), for Twitter-based library services; @jimallthetime and @shroppiemon for help with Shrewsbury history; Zoe Neale; Claire Crossdale (yay Pontefract cakes!); Talia Schaffer, for kindly allowing me to reference her work on Stoker and Wilde; Lesley A. Hall (lesleyahall.net), an absolute font of historical medical information; London School of Hygiene & Tropical Medicine, particularly the lovely Glyn Green; the 'Freedom' internet-blocker app, the use of which is the only way I ever get any work done.

Acknowledgements

Li Zakovics, Lucy Chamberlain – I genuinely wouldn't be here without you and I can never thank either of you enough for how you've kept me upright; Jamie Molloy, who talks as much as I do; Susie Cavill and Roi Robertson, my beloved monsters; Mags, for helping with the maths; Sam Cleasby; Jo Austin and Miriam Barber, two of my favourite idiots; Sheena Lees and Emma Barnard, punners extraordinaire; Ruth Douglas; Louisa Burnham; the Hoors, who know who they are; Birgitta Zoutman and Fran Hansen, for keeping me sane even when they weren't always managing it themselves; CW; BMC and all who sail(ed) in her.

Scott Wheeldon, who inherited most of the brains in the family even if he doesn't always realise it; my father, who died before I could tell him I was writing this book, but who would have been beside himself with pride and pleasure (whilst also lecturing me on the bits he thought I was getting wrong); my mother, who is amazing and brilliant (although how we have managed to not kill each other – yet – is beyond me); Speedy Nan, who has been a constant presence throughout; Marilyn Miller; Boo, who always understands; Amelia Benge, for keeping me entertained when I needed it most; everyone who supported, encouraged and loved me during a period of my life that had all the charisma of a liquified squirrel. I adore you all. Yes, even you.

And above all, my wonderful boys, Jaime and Oscar. Thank you for not judging me when I talk about syphilis during dinner and for knowing how to make a decent G&T. I love you both beyond words.

This book was powered by Lavazza coffee and the music of Nick Cave.

Preface

I've been infatuated with the Victorians throughout my life. Invariably portrayed as being prudish and prim, there was something about them that made me suspect that wasn't quite the case in reality. It's too easy to look back on times past with our knowing, twenty-first century gaze and assume that we're the first generation to be fully accepting of differences in fashion, sexual persuasion, personal morals etc. In reality, we're nothing of the kind: there is as much judgment today as there was a century and a half ago, and the media, if anything, is even more prurient than it was when Victoria was on the throne.

The nineteenth century was just *so* sexy. The very buttoned-up-ness of it makes one think of doomed love affairs, heaving bosoms and tragic endings; everything I've always loved in a story. Artists were pushing the boundaries of sexual depictions in polite society; upstanding gentlemen were writing secret diaries about their innermost desires; even the lowliest of the populace gave thought to illicit desires and sexual pleasure.

Growing up as a child in Shropshire, in a boring, semi-rural market town that sometimes felt cut off from the rest of the world, I would lose myself in endless reruns of old Universal horror movies. I consumed them avidly while clutching my beloved, tattered copy of *Dracula*, wishing fervently that I was one of the terrified-but-plucky heroines, fighting back against the looming threat while also wanting nothing more than to give in and feel those sharp fangs entering my delicate, pale neck. During daylight I had to admit, even to myself, that in reality, I was a maudlin, slightly chubby teenager with a propensity for too much black lace and white panstick that didn't quite suit her; but after dark I could be anything I pleased. Considering how much I looked down on my hometown's apparent dullness, you can imagine how excited my adult self was to discover that the quiet streets where I hung out with friends in the 1980s actually had a dark history of their own. Brothels, steep, narrow lanes with names that could not be uttered in polite company, a dedicated 'penitentiary for outcast women'; Shrewsbury had it all. I have relayed some of its history in these pages with great glee, and can only apologise to my fellow residents. See it less as 'bringing down the tone' and more as 'proving that your ancestors were probably up to the same as you are, if not more'.

I have selfishly focused on the places I love, but hopefully used them to illustrate how similar people really were, across both social and geographical divides. I have a deep and abiding affection for Liverpool in particular, and if any readers have further stories about its Victorian history, please do get in touch. Likewise, Highgate Cemetery in north London. Much as I love all graveyards and cemeteries, Highgate really stands head and shoulders above the rest. The stories behind it – and the people who love and care for it – are valuable beyond measure.

As an era, Victoria's reign included so many massive changes in society that it would have been an impossible task to include them all here. I could easily have written an entire book on each individual topic. There are bound to be omissions and I can only beg forgiveness. Rather like Alice when she entered Wonderland, it's far too easy to get lost down a rabbit hole of curiosity and find yourself distracted by the endless array of new and interesting things, no doubt treading on some equally significant facts while skipping along in excitement. Some dates and places cannot be easily confirmed, but I have researched as well as I can and been honest about things I don't know.

I adore 'my' Victorians. And I hope you will too.

Violet Fenn, Shrewsbury,
March 2019

Introduction

An Era of Sin and Censure

Our endless fascination with the people and events of the nineteenth century is perhaps unsurprising. Between Victoria's coronation and her death, society in Britain underwent many changes. Some of these were already well underway by the time the new, young queen took the throne in 1837. The first Industrial Revolution had begun in the late 1700s and was rapidly picking up pace, its technological advancements forcing society to adapt in order to keep up. The advent of mechanised spinning in the late eighteenth century turned textile production into an industry, which in turn had a major effect on the way people lived, worked and dressed.

Victoria was only eighteen years old when she came to the throne and was almost certainly expected to be little more than a pawn in the games of others. It must have been an unpleasant shock to many in the upper echelons of British society, then, when this young woman turned out to have rather more grit and determination that anyone might have anticipated.

Victoria's first act of independence was to move her overbearing mother out of her way. Princess Victoria of Saxe-Coburg-Saalfeld, Duchess of Kent, had closely supervised her daughter's every move throughout her life so far. She clearly had visions of continuing to do so, thus giving herself de facto control of the country. Her partner in crime was the comptroller of her household, Sir John Conroy, who himself had ambitions of becoming the power behind the throne. Between them, Conroy and the duchess had organised Victoria's cloistered upbringing in Kensington Palace in such a way that the young girl barely came into contact with other children, let alone the royal court: Victoria wasn't even permitted to attend the coronation of her uncle, King William IV.

This strict regime, which became known as the 'Kensington System', was designed so that the young Victoria would be dependent on her guardians for advice and guidance. Such was their level of control over Victoria's activities that she wasn't allowed to use a staircase without a second person holding her hand for safety at all times. She even shared a bedroom with her mother, right up until the moment she became queen.

One can only assume that the young Victoria had been quietly – and resentfully – biding her time. As soon as she took the throne, her mother was summarily evicted from the palace into separate accommodation a few streets away in Belgrave Square. Without the duchess shadowing the queen's every move, Conroy's power also weakened, leaving Victoria free to make her mark across a burgeoning empire.

Victoria also changed her name. Baptised Alexandrina in honour of her godfather, Emperor Alexander I of Russia, Victoria was her middle name, after her mother. Documents written on the first day of Victoria's reign refer to the new queen as Alexandrina, but the name was then withdrawn at her request and never used again.

The new queen's personal beliefs, style and life choices impacted across the entirety of what became the largest empire the world had ever known. Growing into a formidable matriarch – more of a mother to her country in many ways than to her own biological children, and described by some as 'The Grandmother of Europe' – Victoria could be cruel and capricious, subjecting both her family and her court to her whims, regardless of the impact on others. The queen never fully recovered from her beloved Albert's death from typhoid at the relatively young age of forty-two. Her lingering melancholy forced a sense of the deepest grief onto her entire empire, keeping her from public duties for far longer than the two years usually allocated to mourning.

But Britain was moving on and it wasn't going to wait for royal crises to subside. Industrialism and romanticism fought a running battle throughout the century with writers, poets and artists alike attempting to fend off the looming threat of the dark satanic mills via the medium of oil paint and tales of chivalry.

The nineteenth century was a time of rules and regulations, with the State as overlord and endless guidelines for living one's life in the most civilised and moralistic way possible. Inevitably, what was deemed morally and socially acceptable depended almost entirely upon one's status in life and – much more importantly – who might be watching. Many of the most outwardly judgmental of men – and it was almost always men, with a few notable exceptions – hid darker desires and secrets under their starched shirts. This isn't to say that women didn't possess such urges, but female sexuality was repressed so firmly by nineteenth-century 'rules' that undoubtedly much of the mass female libido was sublimated into more socially acceptable activities. Many of the Victorian upper classes lived by the simple principle of 'do as I say, not as I do', whilst the up-and-coming middle class fought for bland, careful respectability.

However polite and proper the Victorians may have appeared in public, there can be no doubt that they were highly sexualised under their stiff and prim exteriors. A society so outwardly buttoned up cannot fail to be seething with desire below the surface, their carnal urges hidden beneath layers of manners and decorum. That same society was in the midst of a swell of cultural change and scientific development. Its curiosity was piqued and its taste for adventure unquenched.

Sex was no different. The rapid changes that took place in society during the Victorian era gave people the courage to question the status quo and begin to wonder just why they should be kept from indulging in things they really wanted to do. And as we all know, being prevented from doing something generally makes us want it all the more. A proportion of the Victorian intellectual classes worked around these restrictions by medicalising sexuality. If you could claim a sexual interest to be purely for the benefit of scientific research – however voyeuristic it now appears to our knowing modern eyes – then you were more likely to be seen as an academic rather than a pervert. The result of over-formalising a natural human response, however, is the development of damaging psychological hang-ups revolving around completely normal sexual behaviour. Real life doesn't, and didn't, fit neatly into the pseudo-scientific boxes that the medically minded intellectuals had developed and were determined to stick to at all costs. After all, ran the academic argument, what upstanding moral citizen would actually *want* to have sex? Well, lots of them, in reality, and considering that it is such a natural part of human life, sex could be a very complicated business.

But industrial progress was coming to the aid of the carnally minded. The rapid development of commercial printing presses enabled faster and broader dissemination of discoveries, beliefs and theories, and the newspapers of the day were always ready and willing to give their biased opinions on society's activities. The increase in travel opportunities via the new rail networks, rapidly connecting towns and cities to the many ports that were growing like barnacles around the coastline, allowed the British population to move around, both at home and abroad, in a way that had never before been possible. The population of Britain, estimated at 12,424,120 in 1811, had risen to 21,121,967 by 1851 (figures vary widely in the early days of census returns; these estimates are from reports collated by the Royal Statistical Society of London). During Victoria's reign British cities, fed by the advance of industry, swelled and spread across the country, overwhelming any smaller towns and villages in their paths and sucking them in to become suburban satellites.

Society was changing at such speed that the government could barely keep pace. New legislation would be brought in hurriedly to quell problems developing unexpectedly, but with a lack of time to finesse the finer details it was often enacted with an overly heavy hand. Laws intended to protect certain vulnerable sections of the population often had the unfortunate side effect of others being demonised or driven underground. Those in the upper echelons, who were in theory responsible for the wellbeing of those below them, often had little working knowledge of how other people's lives were lived in reality.

Luckily for us as a species, humans are incredibly resourceful under pressure, and none more so than those scrabbling for survival at the bottom of the heap. The levels of poverty in nineteenth-century Britain were shocking by any standards, but it doesn't follow that the poor had no time for indulging their intimate urges. To the poverty-stricken lower classes of Victorian Britain, sex was often a (literally) pressing matter. Forced to live cheek by jowl in order to get by, many had little or no physical protection or financial safety net. If you were a poor young woman in nineteenth-century Liverpool, for example, there would almost certainly come a time when you would have little option but to at least consider selling your body to the endless sailors and travellers arriving into the expanding docks via the increasingly busy new trade routes. Better some coins in your pocket or a warm bed for the night than to be left shivering out in the cold of Lime Street with no idea of where your next meal might be coming from.

Those with a safe, secure roof over their heads and servants in the basement didn't necessarily have it any easier in the emotional stakes, even if they were better catered for physically. Despite an emerging awareness of, and desire for, bodily (and political) autonomy, Victorian women were still, in essence, chattels under the ownership of their husbands and/or male relatives. For much of the nineteenth century even a women with her own inherited fortune had to sign it over to her husband upon marriage, with a fervent hope that he could be trusted to care for her from then on. Middle- and upper-class women still had to live by the rules and accept that their lives would be restricted enormously by the strictures of social etiquette. If they didn't play the game correctly, they risked being shunned, both by society and their own families.

Looking back from the present, we also have to take into consideration the huge differences in social attitudes. Nearly two hundred years has passed since Victoria came to the throne, and in that time many generally accepted beliefs have changed almost beyond recognition.

A prime example of the shift in public attitudes since the nineteenth century is the very different view of what constituted an adult as opposed to a child. The age of consent had been set at twelve in 1275 and stayed unchanged until the Offences Against The Person Act 1875, which raised it to thirteen. To our eyes, a thirteen-year-old is very much still a child, but the Victorians hadn't heard of the word 'teenager' and anyone over the age of twelve was simply a young adult. These legal facts don't make it any easier to read about nineteenth-century prostitutes dying of syphilis before they had even hit their mid-teens, but it does mean that we need to remember how different both the moral and legal framework were at the time.

Another theory that fails to stand up to statistical investigation is the idea that life expectancy rates were depressingly low in the 1800s. Certainly in 1841 – the earliest year for which the Office for National Statistics holds data – the 'average' lifespan in Britain was rather short. A man could apparently hope to survive for 40.2 years, whilst, with a bit of luck and a good tail wind, a woman might live to reach the ripe old age of 42.2. These figures, however, are skewed precisely because they are averages. The mortality rate in infants and young children was so high during this period that it brings the general average down hugely. For this reason the ONS also gives modal – 'most frequent' – figures, which discount any deaths under the age of ten years old. These statistics show that if you survived the dangers of childhood you then had a reasonable chance of making it to your sixties, seventies or even older: modal life expectancy in 1841 was seventy-one for males and seventy-seven for females. Of course, this depended on your level of income and your standard of living, as well as whether you managed to avoid contracting cholera, syphilis or any one of the myriad other common nasties lurking round the corner waiting to surprise you in the years before the benefit of vaccination was discovered.

A lack of written or photographic evidence makes it easy to assume that nothing much of titillating interest happened in the nineteenth century. But we have to remember that it is rare for potentially embarrassing (or illegal) vices to be indulged publicly, let alone made a matter of record. Even in today's age of omnipresent cameras and social media, the scandals we hear about can only ever be the tiniest tip of an enormous sexual iceberg.

Combine this natural human reticence with living in an era of careful public manners and social rigidity and you begin to understand why Victorian sexual desires and fantasies were more often kept in the safety of one's head, rather than written down on paper. The fact that the Victorians didn't leave records of what they were getting up to doesn't equate to them never getting up to it.

We now live in a society that often values public interest and third-party approval above an individual's personal happiness and we have to bear in mind that previous generations – not just the poor, beleaguered Victorians – didn't feel the need to share every last detail of their lives with the general public. They were often far too busy simply trying to survive.

The modern perception of Victorians as a staid society that disapproved of pretty much anything that might be enjoyable was created from the hangover of the very last years of Victoria's reign. By the late 1800s she was a stout, elderly woman who was entrenched in deep mourning. This professional widow often showed bitterness towards the happiness of others, particularly that of her own children. Society had spent much of the century enjoying increasingly licentious freedom, to the point that, as the *fin de siècle* reached its final curtain call, the powers that be felt forced into taking a rather heavy-handed stand against what they saw as the development of dangerous immorality.

As public opinion became increasingly clouded by moral judgment, popular culture also began to lead people towards a more restrained way of living. Oscar Wilde was imprisoned for behaviour that today would (mostly) go unremarked upon, save perhaps for a few sly comments in a tabloid gossip column. Jack the Ripper's short but horrifically bloody rampage through the East End of London gave the increasingly powerful newspaper industry endless grimly titillating headlines, and their readers the opportunity to pass voyeuristic judgment on the tragic victims. The rise of the Gothic novel brought us an undead count who imbued the term 'fatal attraction' with a new and deadly meaning, and Alice fell down her rabbit hole, kick-starting an enduring fascination as to the true motives of her creator.

Victoria's death just after the turn of the twentieth century ushered in the Edwardians, often seen as a brief period of joyful licentiousness between the censorious nineteenth century and the horrors created by Victoria's own grandchildren as they pitted their countries against each other in the Great War. But, if anything, it was the advent of the Edwardian era that stoked the fires of class divide, as the rich enjoyed new freedoms while the living conditions of the poor trailed behind. To the working classes and the poverty stricken, life stayed much the same.

In this book, we'll look at how an obsession with masturbation led to (apparent) tragedy, which, in turn, led to huge strides forward in public knowledge of sexual health and contraception; how the diaries of a lowly housemaid show us just how broad-minded and sexually accepting Victorians could be, even when divided by class barriers; and why the tabloid frenzy surrounding the supposed kidnapping of a young girl for the sex trade eventually led to the downfall of one of history's most notorious writers: all against a background of sex-related scandals involving some of the highest – and lowest – in the land.

These, then, are the Victorians. And they are sexier than you might expect.

Author's Note: where possible, I have kept to contemporary terminology when it comes to describing the sexual proclivities of the Victorian era. Some of these descriptions may seem jarring – or even potentially offensive – to modern sensibilities, but are essential for accuracy. We must be careful to view previous eras through a contemporary lens, rather than with the judgment of modern insight.

Chapter 1

Hustle and Bustle

The Unwritten Rules of Fashion and Courtship

Fashion has played a major role in courtship throughout history. Types of fabric, varying styles, and even the colour of clothing has always been a signifier of someone's status in life, and an identifier of what kind of person they are; or, more likely, what kind of person they would like others to *think* they are. Practicality also comes into the mix. Luxuriously tailored outfits with long, dragging hems not only cost more to create and purchase, they indicate (even now) that the person wearing them probably doesn't have to worry too much about the cleaning bills.

Cultural tastes shift in tandem with the political climate, the economy, and the physical wellbeing of the populace itself. If plague or cholera is ripping through your neighbourhood then personal priorities mean that you're less likely to spend time worrying about which trousers go best with that plaid waistcoat. Equally, when the national culture is more buoyant there is room to experiment and take risks, in clothing as well as finances.

So, what was hot and what was not in Victorian Britain? Before the Industrial Revolution, society was fragmented; the production of commercial goods was localised and lacked extensive variation. But as industry expanded, so did the worldview of the general population. Those with the financial means to do so could travel on the new railway system that was spreading across the country. If people could read, they could find out what was happening elsewhere in the world in the newspapers. Even the illiterate could look at the pictures.

Suddenly, people knew what others were doing, and they also knew what they were wearing. New fashions trickled down through a society that could pick up ideas and make some attempt at recreating them, even if they didn't look quite the same as they had on the advert in the evening paper. Romanticism is often taken to mean literally 'romantic' in the sense that we would understand the word today. But in the early nineteenth

1

century, romanticism still held its original meaning: that of the German *Sturm und Drang* movement of the late 1700s, proponents of which saw aesthetic value in expressing the power of nature and wild beauty. There is precious little of modern romance to be found in the bleak wonder of true romantic art and literature.

Romanticism had a massive influence on Victorian fashions and what people considered attractive in the opposite sex. Sir Walter Scott's *Ivanhoe* had been published in 1819 and proved immensely popular with an audience keen to immerse themselves in tales of chivalry and adventure. Credited with inventing the popular image of Scotland, Scott had been responsible for the state visit of King George IV in 1822 – the first visit north of the border by a reigning British monarch since Charles I's Scottish coronation in 1633 – and in doing so, cemented an enduring image of the Highlands, its people and the kilted national dress.

Novels such as *Ivanhoe* – subtitled *'A Romance'*, in case readers didn't quite get the hint – and poetry by the likes of Percy Bysshe Shelley and Lord Byron had unleashed in the British populace a love of many things that we might ourselves recognise today as being 'romantic' in the modern sense. Armoured knights on powerful horses, medieval myths brought to life and powerful, bearded men (just waiting to sweep a maiden off her feet and into their manly arms) featured heavily.

This fashion for appearing chivalrous and generally macho was reinforced when Queen Victoria married her cousin, Albert of Saxe-Coburg and Gotha, on 10 February 1840. Not overly popular with either the general public or Victoria's own advisors ahead of the wedding (mostly because of his relatively lowly status as second in line to a small German dukedom), Victoria was determined that her country should come to love Albert as much as she did. Ignoring the fact that her husband-to-be had almost zero military experience, two days before the wedding the queen bestowed on him the title of honorary field marshall, the highest rank of the British Army. A bespoke uniform then had to be hastily prepared, in order that Albert might look suitably dashing and authoritative at the ceremony.

Victoria's own choice of gown changed the face of the wedding industry more or less overnight. Although white wedding dresses weren't unheard of before 1840, they were a rarity; and for good reason. In the days before commercial bleaching processes, white was the most difficult colour to achieve; it was also the hardest fabric to keep clean. Only the wealthiest of brides would have been able to afford both the fabric *and* the maintenance required for a white dress. Most brides would have simply worn their 'Sunday best'. Even if they were in a position to buy a dress specifically for their wedding, it would generally be one in a practical style and colour, so that it could be worn again after the event. Red was very popular: not only was the colour considered lucky by some, it was also good at hiding stains. In the days before domestic washing machines, clothes would get very grubby around the collars and cuffs, not to mention the dirt that could get onto them simply by walking down the street.

A white wedding dress was, therefore, more a sign of wealth than a symbol of virginity. The 'purity' angle of white dresses is a relatively recent development and didn't start to fully take hold until the middle of the twentieth century. This cultural construct possibly developed from the historical use of white robes in religious ceremonies, particularly those of the Roman Catholic church.

Victoria's devoted approach to both her new husband *and* his public image, alongside a royal wedding that captured the public's imagination, not only brought her the support of the British people that she so desperately needed, but also gave her subjects a template for their own romantic lives. Their young queen was openly and avidly in love with her handsome consort – a German, yes, but one who was proving to be intelligent and level headed – and her country suddenly had a romantic spring in its step. Even if they couldn't aspire to such a royal lifestyle, Victoria's subjects could at least follow her lead elsewhere. And so the romance of the military bridegroom and his white-clad bride was reinforced.

But what's with all this talk of romance, and handsome chaps who might sweep a girl off her feet? Weren't the Victorians the prudish lot who covered up piano legs for fear that the curving shapes might incite lustful urges? After all, the nineteenth century was one of social propriety and books of manners and etiquette. It doesn't take much of a leap to imagine prudish Victorian society insisting on hiding anything that could be deemed improper in any way.

Sadly for our preconceptions, there is no evidence that any piano ever had its lower regions hidden from view; at least not for reasons of propriety. The legend is actually of American origin rather than British, and almost certainly arose from the writings of one Captain Frederick Marryat, a Royal Navy officer who wrote *Diary in America* about his travels in the United States during the late 1830s.

On visiting a seminary for young ladies in the Niagara Falls area, Marryat was surprised to see the legs of a piano covered with what he described as 'modest little trousers'. His guide allegedly told him that the covers were in order to preserve 'the utmost purity of ideas' amongst the young ladies and Marryat faithfully recorded this explanation. It is now widely believed that the covers were either intended to protect the furniture from dust or damage, or were simply an elaborate joke played by Marryat's hosts on their naive English visitor. But the idea stuck, and people still think of Victorians as 'the ones who got excited by wooden legs'.

In reality, the Victorians were a surprisingly open-minded crowd, who had some interesting ideas as to what constituted having a good time. This was the era of freak shows as entertainment. Nineteenth-century public audiences didn't go in for equality between races, or understanding of physical differences in humans in general. If you were different in any way, you were fair game to be stared at, pointed at and, quite possibly, treated as a second-class citizen worthy only of being looked on as a scientific curiosity.

Conditions for freak show 'exhibits' had improved slightly since Sarah Baartman – the 'Hottentot Venus', a South African woman with overly large buttocks, due to a medical condition – had been paraded around London and Paris in the early 1800s, with guests at private shows free to touch her as they wished ('Hottentot' is now considered an offensive term and is only used here in the context of historical accuracy).

Being on the freak-show circuit was still hard work and not much different to being an animal in a travelling zoo, but the newly science-minded paying public were fascinated by difference of all kinds, especially when it enabled them to look down on others less fortunate than themselves while also convincing themselves that it was simply to assuage academic interest.

Séances were a good excuse for a gentleman to sit in the dark next to an unmarried lady on whom he had his eye. If he was very lucky, their hands might even touch on the ouija board planchette. It might seem strange that a society so strictured by religion would be tolerant of superstition, but in the nineteenth century spiritualism was seen less as dabbling in the occult and more a way of potentially connecting with the dead. Victorians believed such contact brought them a step closer to God and spiritualism became popular across all social classes.

Even the queen herself allegedly became involved in the spiritualist movement. There is, however, some doubt as to the veracity of the popular story that Victoria met with clairvoyant Georgiana Eagle at Osborne House in 1846. Some say this was an attempt to communicate with her beloved Albert, despite the fact that he was still alive and kicking at the time (and would stay that way for another fifteen years).

But, whatever its origins, in 1848 interest in spiritualism really began to grip the nation. American sisters Margaret and Kate Fox came to public attention through their popular séances, during which they claimed to speak to the spirit of a man who had, it was said, been murdered many years earlier in the Fox family home in Hydesville, New York. Their story was reported in newspapers across America and Europe, stoking interest in communicating with the dead.

Fellow American medium Maria B. Hayden helped to kick-start the British spiritualist movement in earnest when she visited from Boston, Massachusetts in October 1852. Hayden charged a guinea per head for attendance at her séances and it wasn't long before others realised the potential earnings to be made from developing an ability to talk to lost loved ones.

However dubious its practices on occasion, spiritualism was something of an inadvertently feminist movement, in that women – with their supposedly softer and more intuitive personalities – were believed to be more receptive to signs and messages from the other side. Because of this, female psychics and clairvoyants were taken seriously and afforded a grudging respect that women of the era otherwise rarely achieved. Women could also attend a séance without risking their behaviour being seen as inappropriate, and men could sit next to them in the dark without a single eyebrow being raised.

Magic shows were another popular destination for those Victorians who wished to partake in an evening's entertainment while also keeping an eye out for potential paramours. Rather less intimate than a séance, these were more akin to cabaret and presented as a pseudo-scientific investigation into hidden powers. Illusionists became immensely popular during the nineteenth century, with such famous stage tricks as 'Pepper's Ghost', first performed in 1862 – which gave the appearance of a ghostly figure appearing in an otherwise normal room – becoming a staple of the music hall circuit. A society living through some of the greatest technological advances in history still wanted to be surprised and shocked by things they didn't understand and the 'Ghost Show' in particular became a perennial favourite.

Courtship was a social maze that had to be navigated with great care in the nineteenth century. There were rules for precisely how a young gentleman might approach a lady who had taken his fancy and, in return, the object of his affections knew she had to respond in specific ways in order to stick to the expected script. Calling cards were an important item of etiquette, though only amongst the middle and upper classes: their use required servants to deliver the cards and also to receive them from visitors on the doorstep. The cards would then be kept in a tray for the mistress of the house to decide at her leisure whether or not to accept the sender for a formal visit at a later date.

In some ways, calling cards were simply the telephones and text messages of their time: they allowed one to proffer the hand of friendship, or possibly romance, while giving the recipient notice of your intent and the chance to decide whether to accept or decline without embarrassment. There were hidden codes related to calling cards: for example, a carefully turned corner on a card indicated that it had been delivered in person rather than by a servant. There was no expectation attached to sending a calling card, although there was, no doubt, often some hope. Only if the gesture was returned with another card could the first person feel confident that their attentions were welcomed.

Victorian courtship was a serious business, with a 'suitable' marriage as the end goal. If a gentleman had received a positive response to the card he left on his initial visit, he would then return for a formal welcome into the house. Any meetings between young people would be closely supervised to ensure that no impropriety took place. If the potential pair decided they liked each other, they might begin 'walking out': literally going for a stroll together, but never touching.

Should a chap see a lady in the street to whom he had previously been introduced, he couldn't simply go up to speak to her. Despite already knowing who the other was, they had to be reintroduced before it was acceptable for them to speak directly to one another. They would then have to attempt to gauge whether they actually liked each other through stilted conversation, invariably in the company of others.

Young ladies of the aristocratic classes would 'come out' as debutantes around the age of sixteen or seventeen and spend the 'season' parading and dancing while keeping a sharp eye out for potential suitors, preferably those with money or property. The richest of the debs, as they came to be known, were presented to the queen at a series of highly formal, highly fashionable 'coming out balls'. Those who were wealthy but not so well bred attended similar events at various grand houses across the country, but didn't get to curtsy to Victoria herself.

Girls were expected to find themselves a husband within the period of three seasons. If they failed in their task they were considered a failure, doomed to live out their days as a spinster and quite possibly seen as a burden to their family. The season was, in effect, a massive social cattle market in which both males and females showed off their most impressive plumage and hoped desperately that they would catch the eye of a suitable match. It was, in a way, like a modern Saturday night down at the local nightclub, though with (marginally) less vomit in the toilets.

The working class had a slightly less formal approach to courtship, but there were still rules to follow; at least in public. The best opportunity to meet the opposite sex would be at the Sunday church service or other similar community events, where brief conversation might be managed, or a shy smile exchanged across a crowded room. Families may have already decided amongst themselves that a particular daughter would make the ideal wife for a son who needed to settle down and make something of his life. The youngsters might find themselves pushed together with an air of expectation and would be hoping that they did indeed take a shine to their suggested partner, in order to keep things as simple as possible. A farmer, getting on in years and in need of a new generation to tend the cattle and plough the fields, might push his eldest son towards the strongest and heartiest of a neighbour's daughters in the hope of them raising a brood of agriculturally-minded grandchildren to keep the family line going.

But not everyone stuck to the rules, even in the upper echelons of society. Lady Florence Paget was a noted society beauty. She was also a woman who wasn't afraid of breaking the rules of polite society in order to get what she wanted. While engaged to the Right Honourable Henry Chaplin, 1st Viscount Chaplin, Florence fell for Chaplin's close friend and great rival, the Marquess of Hastings. In July 1864, the pair eloped by the wonderfully devious method of asking Viscount Chaplin to wait outside Marshall & Snelgrove's department store in London's Oxford Street while Lady Florence bought clothes for their imminent wedding. The errant bride-to-be walked straight through the shop and out the back door, where the Marquess was waiting in his own carriage to whisk her away.

Chaplin would get his revenge against the gambling, drinking Hastings on the racecourse. Both men entered horses in the 1867 Epsom Derby. Chaplin's well-fancied stallion, Hermit, had dropped in the stakes due to health problems in the run-up to the race and Hastings took the opportunity to bet heavily against him. Hermit won, and bankrupted Hastings in the process. Hastings died in poverty the following year, at the age of only twenty-six. His widow went on to marry Sir George Chetwynd, 4th Baronet of Brocton Hall, and bore him a son in 1874 (Florence clearly had a 'type': not only was Chetwynd another racehorse owner and gambler, but after their marriage, on one occasion, he had to be physically separated from Lord Lonsdale in Hyde Park, after the pair scuffled over Lonsdale's companion, Lillie Langtry).

Polite as Victorian society might appear on the surface, it wasn't above indulging in the sharpest of humour at times. 'Vinegar Valentines' were a popular – if rather cruel – joke that started at the beginning of Victoria's reign and carried on into the early part of the twentieth century. An anonymous card would be sent to an unfortunate recipient, detailing in short verse why the sender considered them an appalling person. Available in different themes, depending on your target – a boring man, or a 'fast' woman, maybe – they certainly didn't hold back. In the words of one card aimed at a jilted suitor:

> I'm not attracted by your glitter
> For well I know how very bitter
> My life would be, if I should take
> You for my spouse, a rattlesnake
> Oh no, I'd not accept the ring
> Or evermore 'twould prove a sting

Proof, if proof were needed, that bitchy putdowns existed long before social media. And you had to put in the effort of paying the postage and physically sending it (petty revenge requiring rather more effort in the 1800s).

As society progressed and changed, so did trends in clothing and fashion. The increased development of modern media, in the form of daily newspapers, meant that society and fashion news could be disseminated by an increasingly large audience, all eager to emulate the fashions they saw being worn by the rich and famous. Celebrities existed in the nineteenth century, much as they do today: Lillie Langtry was famed as much for her looks and her relationships with various noblemen (including Prince Bertie, whose very tolerant wife, Princess Alexandra, apparently accepted Lillie's presence in their life) as she was for her acting; and Daisy Greville, Countess of Warwick, was a celebrated hostess as well as the inspiration for the famous music hall song, '*Daisy, Daisy*'.

> There is a flower within my heart, Daisy, Daisy
> Planted one day by a glancing dart
> Planted by Daisy Bell
> Whether she loves me or loves me not,
> Sometimes it's hard to tell;
> Yet I am longing to share the lot
> Of beautiful Daisy Bell
>
> Daisy, Daisy,
> Give me your answer, do
> I'm half crazy,
> All for the love of you
> It won't be a stylish marriage,
> I can't afford a carriage,
> But you'll look sweet on the seat
> Of a bicycle built for two

In the early 1800s the fashion for more complicated gowns was still the province of those who could afford to have clothing made to measure. But during the latter half of the century paper patterns became increasingly available, making it possible for even the lowliest working-class woman to create for herself an approximation of the latest styles.

The early Victorian era was one of layers, and everyone wore a similar style, even if the quality differed. A Victorian woman's first layer would be her underwear. Bloomers/drawers were designed with either an open or closed crotch; and when you realise just how complicated Victorian clothing could be, you begin to understand why the open crotch was so popular. They made it possible to relieve oneself with nothing more than a squat and a hoisting of skirts.

The next layer would be a cotton chemise, which protected the rest of the clothes from natural oils and sweat and was far easier and cheaper to replace when necessary. The chemise was followed by a corset, which almost everyone wore, regardless of status. Corsets had, for a long time, been the preserve of the middle and upper classes, because of the cost of having clothes made to one's own specific measurements. However, with the advent of 'ready to wear' items, the corset – and other fashionable items of clothing – became accessible to all but the very poorest of women.

The hourglass shape that a corset provided was accentuated during the middle of the century by the fashion for 'tight-lacing', the practice of forcing the waist into a rather uncomfortable looking tiny size by the gradual tightening of waist corset. A Victorian woman was not considered properly dressed unless she was trussed up in whalebone and linen like an oven-ready chicken.

This already shapely female silhouette was given even more fullness by the application of several horsehair petticoats, each one stiff and heavy and tied around the waist with its own separate ribbon. Some women wore feather-quilted petticoats for extra volume. Imagine trying to walk around with several duvets tied to your waist and you'll get the idea. Victorian women were not expecting to have to run for a bus. After the invention of crinoline, skirts became lighter, as petticoats were no longer needed to give the bell-like shape that was fashionable. However, crinolines had their own dangers. As they could be used to make skirts wider than ever, there were regular instances of women's clothing catching fire after a crinoline had swung too close to an open fireplace. It was also not unheard of for the wearer to be accidentally stabbed with a steel spring after the boning in a crinoline popped out of its sewn channel in the fabric. It's worth noting that crinolines were particularly disliked in some (male) quarters, for the simple reason that a woman wearing skirt hoops took up a lot of space. Men were being pushed out of the way – literally – by women who dared to wear the new fashions and dared to take up space.

A final outer skirt would button or tie over the petticoats or crinoline frame, usually in a dark colour for practicality's sake as Victorian skirts were long enough to drag on the ground. These were the days long before streets were expected to be clean. Even the upper classes would have no option but to drag their hems through all manner of filth when they stepped out of the house.

The corset would then be covered with a bodice and a fitted jacket would often go over the top. Sometimes the jacket was buttoned down onto the under layers, to make absolutely sure that there would never be an accidental sight of naked flesh. Wealthier women would perhaps add a cape, gloves and even a parasol.

It is easy for us to imagine what appears to be a complicated, many-layered costume and assume that it must have been claustrophobic and difficult to wear. There is also often talk of how women were held hostage to fashion, unable to dress themselves without the help of a maid. Thankfully for our fashionable Victorian ladies, neither of these assumptions are true.

The clothing can certainly seem cumbersome to our eyes, but we live in an era of zips and one-piece clothing and have become used to getting dressed and undressed in seconds. The Victorians were accustomed to their many layers, and more than capable of dressing themselves in not much more time than it takes us today. There were, however, definite safety issues with some aspects of Victorian clothing, not least those caused by the sheer weight of the layers that many women wore. Petticoats were heavy even when dry; if they got wet it could prove fatal.

Author Gill Hoffs has written several books about nineteenth-century shipwrecks and understands more than most just how easily a woman's clothing could become waterlogged, hampering her chances of surviving a disaster at sea, even when they were well within reach of help:

> The luckiest women involved with shipwrecks were stripped of their cumbersome outer layers by menfolk with sharp knives and the time and wit (and elbow-room) to use them to essentially fillet the rows of buttons or strong stitches holding an outfit in place – or did so themselves. Rarer were the women and girls whose skirts and sleeves trapped pockets of air as they reached the waves, effectively allowing them time to be plucked from the water as their clothing acted as a flotation device. It was far more common for those who survived the initial wrecking event to plummet to the depths, legs entangled in bloomers and petticoats, face and arms shrouded in shawls and overskirts. Despite this, many bodies would soon wash up naked or with just

a waistband in place, leading to baseless accusations of plundering by locals but actually just evidence of the sheer might of the sea.

Even if a lady stayed safely on dry land, risks were all around. This was many decades before non-flammable dress fabrics existed and during a time when the majority of lighting still relied on open flames from gas lamps or candles.

Mary and Emily Wilde were the illegitimate daughters of Irish surgeon William Wilde, which made them half-sisters to the infamous Oscar. Although it's not known whether the playwright was ever aware of his half siblings' existence, William acknowledged the girls as his own. He gave them the family name and presumably contributed towards their living costs, as the sisters led a relatively comfortable lifestyle and regularly mixed socially with Irish high society.

On Tuesday, 31 October 1871, Mary and Emily attended a Halloween party at Drumaconnor House near Threemilehouse in County Monaghan. As the party wound to a close, one of the sisters – thought to have been Mary – danced too close to a burning candlestick and her dress caught fire. As the rest of the guests fled in panic, Emily desperately tried to help her sister but her own clothes also caught alight. There are conflicting reports as to what happened next, but the most likely explanation is that the girls managed to run down the stairs and outside, flinging themselves to the ground and rolling in an attempt to put out the flames. Despite somehow surviving the awful incident, both girls suffered extensive third degree burns, before succumbing to their terrible injuries; Mary eventually dying on 9 November and her sister Emily on 21 November.

A Victorian gentleman's dressing process was slightly easier. Isn't that always the way? Let's examine a dapper man in a major British city, circa 1885. The first thing you will notice is his good quality, weather-resistant topcoat, made from a dark merino broadcloth. His notched lapels have a velvet contrast trim and the coat is fitted, dropping to the knee. From what we can see of his trousers, they are a loose fit and come right down to meet his buttoned leather shoes. We know that the trousers will be held up with braces over a fitted cotton shirt with buttoned cuffs, but little is visible underneath his smart, double-breasted waistcoat and the silk necktie that flounces out of his neat collar.

If we were uncouth enough to ask this chap what he had on underneath, the answer would be 'not very much'; certainly not in comparison to the women dragging their heavy skirts along the pavement behind them. Men generally kept to the basics; a vest and drawers, possibly made of flannel. If it was very cold, he might be wearing his 'combinations'; a one-piece undergarment that was literally a combination of drawers and vest, keeping out any chills and ensuring a neat finish to the outfit.

The lower classes would wear much simpler versions of these same outfits, put together from bits and pieces of mismatched clothing bought second-, third- or even fourth-hand. Clothes would be mended and patched and passed down through family members until there was barely anything left of them. In very poor areas, one might resort to buying from a 'picker', someone who stole clothes from the dead and sold them on to anyone desperate enough to ignore the suspicious stains (and probable lice lurking in the fabric). Poor women followed the fashion of wearing hats, as much to protect their hair from dirt and lice as to appear stylish. Clothes would be chosen in dark colours in order to hide dirt for as long as possible in the days before convenient laundry facilities.

No one was exempt from the expectation of basic decency when it came to clothing. Women would wear similar styles and layers, regardless of class or wealth, but the poor would have to scrimp where they could. A working-class Victorian woman might wear fewer petticoats, and her chemise may have been worn by two or three sisters before her. Her clothes may have been patched and threadbare, but she would still have met certain fashion (and moral) requirements, even if she wore no shoes on her feet (those who were lucky enough to have shoes would probably have inherited them from another member of the family and they would be made from heavy wood and leather, possibly with hobnails hammered into the soles).

Even the poor would do their utmost to have one outfit for 'Sunday Best'. This was the cleanest and tidiest ensemble that they could manage, kept to wear to the Sunday church service and for 'walking out' on their one day off work (walking being the main form of entertainment in the days before cable television and nightclubs). Some might have to resort to pawning the outfit first thing on Monday morning in order to feed their family, but they would buy it – or something similar – back again in readiness for the following weekend.

As the century wore on, fashion had to meet the changing needs of a society developing the courage to stretch its social restrictions. Adaptations were made to clothing to enable enthusiastic lady horse riders to pursue their sport with fewer physical limitations. The most notable of these women paraded their steeds along Rotten Row in Hyde Park, a favoured spot for wealthy equestrians to show off their skills and beauty in front of eligible gentlemen (the name is a corruption of the French *Route du Roi*, King's Road).

With the growth of the economy and the associated expansion of the middle and upper classes during the 1800s, the numbers of women taking to the saddle for leisure and pleasure increased exponentially. Women needed dedicated clothes, as their usual skirts and corsets were impractical for riding sidesaddle.

Women had happily sat astride their horses for centuries with barely a thought for supposed decency, until Anne of Bohemia travelled on horseback to England in 1382, in order to marry King Richard II. It was decreed that the soon-to-be-royal hymen had to be protected at all costs, and to that end, poor Anne ended up perched precariously on a small chair with a footrest, which required her to sit completely sideways. This made it impossible to control her horse (or do anything else other than attempt to stay on), which therefore had to be led by a man.

The more secure design of sidesaddle with the double-hooked pommels didn't appear until the 1830s. It still looked rather cumbersome in contrast to the regular saddles used by men, but it did at least give women their equestrian freedom once again. And though it may look precarious, a rider is actually very secure on a sidesaddle and is able to gallop and jump with the best of them.

Ladies were still expected to meet certain sartorial standards of modesty while out riding. Skirts had to be cut differently in order to still look presentable when mounted and were much longer than usual so that they covered the ankles when the rider was in the saddle. This meant that they had to be carried over the arm while on the ground, in order to avoid being dragged through the dirt. Hats would be worn – to protect delicate complexions rather than for safety – and tied with a ribbon under the chin or around the nape of the neck to avoid them flying off while on the move, and they would often have a veil attached to protect the wearer from dirt and dust.

Some women did ride astride on a 'cross-saddle' – a standard riding saddle to most of us – but it was a rarity and generally restricted to only the most thrusting of lady riders out with the hunt. One can only assume that such ladies were less likely to care about the opinions of others (or, more likely, that other people were less likely to have the nerve to criticise them, to their face at least).

The increased enthusiasm for cycling in the late 1800s led to huge changes in women's clothes, as they developed ingenious ways of adapting 'acceptable' fashions in order to be able to enjoy the new freedom that cycling brought with it. Bicycles were an important tool of emancipation for nineteenth-century women, increasingly so as bike design developed into something more akin to modern styles towards the end of the century. As they became more readily available and convenient to ride, the use of bicycles trickled down through society.

Originally available only to the wealthy as a leisure activity, cycling became a favoured mode of transport for the working middle class and literally opened up a new world. Middle-class men began using bicycles for transport to and from work, while women could now justify travelling further than they had previously been able. And given that they were far less easy to supervise while on two wheels, cycling gave women a sense of freedom that they'd never had before.

Inevitably, there was a backlash against female cyclists – or 'wheelers' as they were sometimes known – from those who considered the activity to be somehow unladylike. It even was feared (invariably by men) that women might obtain sexual arousal from sitting astride the cycle seat, with some bicycles having a cut-out seat to avoid pressure on any dangerously sensitive areas. A form of 'side saddle' cycle was even developed, but unsurprisingly proved cumbersome and unstable.

It was argued from some quarters that women might give birth to malformed babies should they cycle while pregnant. And, of course, there was the dreaded 'Bicycle Face', a supposed disease caused by cycling which left the unfortunate sufferer with a misshapen head complete with scrunched up eyes, sagging jaw line and a rather bemused expression. Physician Arthur Shadwell, the person responsible for 'inventing' Bicycle Face, had other dire warnings for female would-be cyclists: 'In case within my knowledge a girl developed exophthalmic goitre* as the result of a rather long ride, which she supposed herself able to accomplish without difficulty. Her throat swelled at the time, never went down, and quickly developed into a well-marked case. This obscure but serious affection is said to be chiefly caused by "mental excitement".' *Now known as

15

Graves' Disease, 'exophthalmic goitre' is an endocrine disorder, which causes hypothyroidism (and a distinct swelling in the throat).

Such fearmongering was, of course, nothing more than a thinly disguised attempt at keeping women in their place within society, i.e. below men and with fewer freedoms. It didn't work: women had tasted freedom on wheels and they weren't going to give it up.

The increase in female cyclists helped in no small part to finally kill off the fashion for corsets, as they were utterly impractical when on two wheels. The full and heavy-layered skirts that had been *de rigeur* for decades made cycling impossible, so adaptations had to be made. Women who had previously taken for granted that they were obliged to ensure they were covered from neck to ankle at all times, with skirts billowing around them, suddenly realised that it might make sense to wear (still very loose and all-encompassing) trousers when cycling, to avoid becoming entangled in the spokes.

Changes in clothing didn't stop some manufacturers attempting to appeal to those who still felt obliged to fit certain polite standards while cycling. Starley Bros were the Coventry bicycle manufacturers whose invention of the 'safety bike' in 1885 saved so many from struggling with the ungainly 'ordinary' cycles (what we now know as penny farthings). In 1889 Starley brought out the rather wonderfully named 'Psycho Ladies Cycle'. With a step-through frame that was low enough for a lady to sit astride without hoisting her skirts, the Psycho enabled even the most prim of Victorian ladies to ride out without flashing those tempting ankles.

The humble bicycle, in its own small way, helped to change forever women's place in society, both in Britain and abroad. American suffragette, Susan B. Anthony, wrote in 1896: 'I think it has done more to emancipate women than anything else in the world.'

There were some rather more formal attempts to bring about more equality in fashion. The Rational Dress Society was formed in London in 1881, with the following aims:

> The Rational Dress Society protests against the introduction of any fashion in dress that either deforms the figure, impedes the movements of the body, or in any way tends to injure the health. It protests against the wearing of tightly-fitting

corsets; of high-heeled shoes; of heavily-weighted skirts, as rendering healthy exercise almost impossible; and of all tie down cloaks or other garments impeding on the movements of the arms. It protests against crinolines or crinolettes of any kind as ugly and deforming....[It] requires all to be dressed healthily, comfortably, and beautifully, to seek what conduces to birth, comfort and beauty in our dress as a duty to ourselves and each other.

The Society counted Constance Wilde – wife of Oscar – as a member, alongside the inventor of the 'divided skirt', Florence Pomeroy, Viscountess Harberton. Pomeroy also founded the 'Short Skirts League', whose daring members would go out walking in skirts that finished a salacious five inches from the ground.

In 1889 fervent Rational Dress activist Charlotte Stopes (eventually to become mother of Marie Stopes, founder of the family planning charity) made a speech at the British Association for the Advancement of Science. Charlotte was a last-minute addition to the list of speakers and her thoughts were considered controversial enough to make the newspapers across the country. According to a report in the *Newcastle Evening Chronicle*, Stopes's speech received a positive reaction from its surprised audience, her resolution being carried to great applause.

Perhaps surprisingly, not all women supported the idea of fashionable advancement for the fairer sex. Eliza Lynn Linton was the first formally salaried female journalist in Britain, but wrote from a decidedly anti-feminist viewpoint. Linton held particular disdain for those who the media were calling 'New Women'; those pushing for gender equality and emancipation. In her essay 'The Girl of the Period', published in the *Saturday Review* in 1868, Linton avowed:

It leads to slang, bold talk and general fastness; to the love of pleasure and indifference to duty; to the desire of money before either love or happiness; to uselessness at home, dissatisfaction with the monotony of ordinary life, horror of all useful work; in a word, to the worst forms of luxury and selfishness – to the most fatal effects arising from want of high principle and absence of tender feeling.

17

Neither did she hold back on what she perceived as the New Woman's failures when it came to marriage:

> The legal barter of herself for so much money, representing so much dash, so much luxury and pleasure – that is her idea of marriage; the only idea worth entertaining. For all seriousness of thought respecting the duties or the consequences of marriage, she has not a trace. If children come, they find but a step-mother's cold welcome from her; and if her husband thinks that he has married anything that is to belong to him [...] the sooner he wakes from his hallucination and understands that he has simply married someone who will condescend to spend his money on herself, and who will shelter her indiscretions behind the shield of his name, the less severe will be his disappointment.

Linton remained convinced in her views, even doubling down on her opinions in a preface written twenty years later:

> I am more than ever convinced that I have struck the right chord of condemnation, and advocated the best virtues and most valuable characteristics of women. I neither soften nor retract a line of what I have said. One of the modern phases of womanhood – hard, unloving, mercenary, ambitious, without domestic faculty and devoid of healthy natural instincts – is still to me a pitiable mistake and a grave national disaster.

Chapter 2

Beddings, Weddings and Bastards

Virginity, Pre-Marital Sex and
the Curse of Illegitimacy

Virginity and innocence – or at least, the appearance of them – were important virtues in Victorian Britain. Women and girls were in effect chattels, belonging to first their fathers and, later, their husbands. Their social value could drop dramatically should they be seen to be behaving in an unladylike manner. This included such crimes as being caught alone with a man, or even just talking to one without supervision.

Middle- and upper-class women were generally chaperoned so closely that they were unlikely to ever be in a position to have sex before marriage, even had they wanted to. In addition, the risk of bringing shame on the family name – and, in the process, ruining one's own chances in life – were just too great a risk. But working-class girls – or those who simply lived in poverty – led rather less structured lives. Although still supervised, a lower-class girl would more often be chaperoned by a relative; perhaps a sibling, who could potentially be bribed to turn a blind eye when their sister wanted to meet her sweetheart for a sneaky cuddle while out on a pleasant morning walk.

Girls were still expected to 'save' themselves for marriage, though it is unlikely that everyone kept to this rule. The important thing was less about abstaining completely and more about simply not getting caught. Perhaps surprisingly, pre-marital sex was, under certain circumstances, more acceptable in the nineteenth century than we often assume, particularly within the lower classes. Certainly, once a couple had announced their engagement, intimacy was considered more acceptable, the betrothal being considered a publicly declared intention to wed.

But this was still strictly on the condition that you didn't get caught; or worse, get pregnant. 'Not getting pregnant' wasn't something people knew much about in the nineteenth century, at least not usually to a helpfully practical extent. Even if you were pragmatic enough to understand that certain preventative measures could be taken, contraception was generally seen as a crime against God in a society that was still heavily tied to religious beliefs. In addition, it wasn't particularly reliable.

A pregnant, unmarried woman was very vulnerable indeed. But, even then, she could be saved, if the man responsible agreed to marriage, thus 'making an honest woman' of her. It's likely that some marriages were based on nothing more than pragmatic convenience. The husband didn't necessarily have to be the father of the child, so long as he either believed he was, or was happy to go along with the conceit; possibly in return for a handsome payment from the girl's own (presumably very relieved) father.

In a surprisingly progressive move, Victorian women also had the option of suing for 'breach of promise' should a lover leave them in the lurch. Taking this option was, in effect, a tacit admission that sexual intercourse had taken place and that the woman had then been abandoned with her reputation potentially in tatters. Some women even chose this path despite not actually being pregnant, in order to save what was left of their reputation. The lower classes in particular often lived cheek by jowl, which meant that others around them would inevitably know when an intimate relationship was being conducted in the vicinity. They would generally reserve their judgement, but only so long as honour was seen to be upheld.

The introduction of the Poor Law Act, enacted during the reign of Victoria's predecessor King William IV in 1834, had absolved fathers of any responsibility towards 'bastard' children; those illegitimate babies born out of wedlock. Unmarried mothers also received less support than before, supposedly as a deterrent against getting pregnant in the first place. The only thing this change succeeded in doing was to make life even harder for those women who got caught out. The poor were particularly vulnerable; some masters would take advantage of servants, only to fire them and throw them out onto the streets when it became apparent that they were in the family way.

Woe betide the girl who got pregnant out of wedlock and was abandoned. The instinct of many of these poor girls would have been to attempt to end the pregnancy before anyone recognised her condition. Her options were limited, but they did exist. Abortion wasn't technically illegal in

Britain until the beginning of the nineteenth century; up until then it had generally been viewed as an unpleasant but sometimes necessary procedure. The rather misleadingly-titled 'Malicious Shooting or Stabbing Act' of 1803 made abortion a criminal offence for the first time:

> An Act for the further Prevention of malicious shooting, and attempting to discharge loaded Fire-Arms, stabbing, cutting, wounding, poisoning and the malicious using of Means to procure the Miscarriage of Women; and also the malicious setting Fire to Buildings; and also for repealing a certain Act, made in the twenty-first Year of the late King James the First, intituled, An Act to prevent the destroying and murthering of Bastard Children; and also an Act made in Ireland in the sixth Year of the Reign of the late Queen Anne, also intituled, An Act to prevent the destroying and murthering of Bastard Children; and for making other Provisions in lieu thereof. [sic]

One can only wonder at the rather arbitrary combination of crimes that were included in the Act. Regardless of the somewhat confused wording, the Act made it a crime for the first time to procure or carry out an abortion. Potential punishment depended entirely on how far along the woman's pregnancy had advanced before it had been ended. Termination before 'quickening' – the point at which the mother feels the unborn child move for the first time – carried a term of fourteen years transportation, while those convicted of post-quickening abortions were liable for the death penalty. At the time, it was generally believed that the foetus was not 'alive' until quickening had occurred.

Regardless of its criminal status, abortion did not go away; it merely went further underground.

The term 'diachylon' was originally used to describe a herbal remedy made from plant juice. But by the 1800s, it generally referred to 'lead-plaster': plaster made from a mixture of lead oxide, oil and water. A spate of miscarriages amongst the population of Sheffield in the late 1800s was traced to lead that had leached into the water supply from the city's metal pipes. It wasn't long before women realised that, if they were lucky, they might be able to bring on their 'missing period' by drinking a watered-down solution of diachylon. An article in the *Lancet* in 1898 reported the story of a twenty-eight-year-old woman who, in the course of being treated for lead poisoning, admitted to having taken 'stuff' to bring on a miscarriage.

Diachylon was, at the time, a common item in the store cupboards of many working-class homes. Available as a paste, it was ready-applied to fabric strips and stored for use in the same way as we would today use sticking plasters. It didn't take much effort to scrape the paste from the fabric, stir it into water and consume as a fairly effective (but presumably deeply unpleasant tasting) abortifacient. Of course, using diachylon also came with the inherent risk of developing lead poisoning, as the poor woman in the *Lancet* report had discovered, but this was clearly a risk worth taking.

Other methods of solving the pregnancy problem included the ubiquitous 'lots of gin and a hot bath', or perhaps risking throwing oneself down a stairwell; all in the hope of causing enough damage to abort the foetus without killing the poor woman. An even more drastic option would be to visit a backstreet abortionist, with all the risks of infection and physical damage that it entailed. There was no such thing as sterilised medical equipment. Furthermore, a Victorian abortionist would care more about getting the job done quickly and the unfortunate woman back out of the door than they would about protecting the patient's health and safety.

If a woman's attempts at inducing or procuring an abortion failed then she had no option but to carry the child to term and manage the best she could. The official rates of illegitimate births are relatively low in the nineteenth century, but the figures are unlikely to be correct and it's far more likely that illegitimacy was simply well hidden. A desperate new mother might well have considered infanticide to be the only way out, perhaps even believing it was better for the child to die immediately rather than face a lifetime of being a poverty-stricken outcast. There were 203 cases of infanticide brought before the judges at the Old Bailey during the nineteenth century, though the actual figures were almost certainly higher. Considering how relatively common stillbirths were, a mother could claim to have given birth to an already-dead child, and it would be almost impossible to prove anything different.

The strain of trying both to survive and look after a baby without financial support also ran the risk of tipping a fragile new mother over into a mental health crisis. For much of the nineteenth century, courts showed surprising leniency towards mothers who had killed their newborns, declaring them as suffering 'puerperal insanity' (postpartum psychosis) and committing them to a local asylum rather than to jail. Some of these women may genuinely have been suffering from what we would now call puerperal psychosis, but as psychosis is a true medical emergency – and current research suggests that it affects only one tenth of one per cent of women who give birth – it's more likely that many instances were cases of infanticide in the face of few alternative options.

Ironically, it was a case of almost certainly genuine psychosis that tipped public opinion against giving such women the benefit of the doubt. On the night of Tuesday, 22 August 1865, forty-one-year-old Esther Lack slit the throats of three of her four children while her husband was out working as a night watchman. Her only surviving child, George, told the Old Bailey, 'Christopher was lying on the bed [...] there was blood all over his face [...] I could not see what had caused his death [...] I saw that my sisters' throats were cut [...] I stood on the stairs crying.' There was other evidence to suggest that Esther had serious mental health issues and the court duly found her not guilty on the grounds of insanity. This was too much for some newspapers, who questioned the leniency of the legal system in such cases.

If the new mother couldn't bring herself to hurt her child, she might attempt to find it an adoptive home. Of course, this depended on having the time to search for suitable prospective parents, and often women in such a situation needed as quick a fix as possible. The next best option to arranging adoption personally was to pay a kindly person – almost always a woman – to keep the baby in her care until she herself could find a suitable adoptive home for it. Thus could the mother leave her responsibilities behind, go back to her old life, and pretend the child had never existed.

Unfortunately, life often wasn't quite so simple for the babies left behind. The unlicensed adoption trade became known as baby farming – a term coined by the *London Times* in the 1860s – and it attracted more than its fair share of unscrupulous people who thought nothing of neglecting or even murdering their charges in order to make room for the next poor mites whose mothers were desperately seeking a kind home for them.

Evelina Marmon was one such mother. A twenty-five-year-old barmaid from Cheltenham, Evelina gave birth to an illegitimate daughter on 21 January 1896 and named her Doris. Luckier than some in her predicament, Evelina's landlady had allowed her to stay in her lodgings while pregnant, but now that little Doris had arrived her young mother needed to make more permanent arrangements. When Doris was two months old, Evelina spotted an advert in the *Bristol Times and Mirror*: 'Couple, with no child, want care of or will adopt one. Terms £10'.

While it might seem incredible now that women were prepared to hand over their newborn child to complete strangers based on nothing but blind trust and forced by panic, the nineteenth century was a different world. Evelina Marmon clearly thought she was doing the best for her tiny baby girl. On Tuesday, 31 March she wrapped Doris in a woollen cloak and blankets and packed some extra nappies and clothes, before setting off to meet 'Mrs Harding' at Gloucester railway station. The baby was handed over, with the apparently affectionate new adoptive mother promising to keep in touch and inviting Evelina to visit whenever she wished.

Evelina never saw her daughter again. Doris's tiny body was recovered from the Thames on Friday, 10 April by the police, who had been dragging the river for evidence during the previous few weeks after the discovery of several other infant bodies. Doris had been strangled within hours of leaving her mother's arms and packed into a carpet bag, along with clothing, bricks and another dead child, later identified as thirteen-month-old Harry Simmons.

Amelia Dyer made her living by taking in the offspring of women who couldn't care for them, usually because of illegitimacy. Dyer took payment from the mothers to cover the costs of looking after their babies and then sent the young women on their way, reassuring them that their child would be cared for. She then almost immediately strangled the child with a length of white tape. This was her trademark and she would later tell police it was 'how you could tell it was one of mine'. The mother's money would go straight into Dyer's own pocket, and any belongings that the baby had arrived with were pawned.

Dyer became the most notorious baby farmer of them all. Now believed to have been responsible for more than four hundred child murders, she was sentenced to death and hanged at Newgate Prison on Wednesday, 10 June 1896. When asked if she had any last words, Dyer simply replied, 'I have nothing to say.'

A marginally luckier expectant mother might manage to get her child accepted by a foundling hospital. The very fact that these hospitals had been established may have been a form of official acknowledgement of the dire straits many women found themselves in, but it was an extremely strict and judgmental one.

The foundling hospitals had self-imposed high moral standards and would only take the offspring of those women and girls deemed 'suitable', despite the mothers themselves never coming under the hospitals' care. The mother would be interviewed and the circumstances of her pregnancy taken into account. Those apparent innocents who were believed to have been taken advantage of by the wiles of devious men were likely to have their babies accepted, but if a girl was deemed to have acted improperly – if she had been seen entering a man's lodgings alone, perhaps, or had simply looked a little bit too cheerful about being in male company – then her child risked being rejected as unsuitable and left to the destitute mother's tender mercies.

The lower classes were the most likely to end up in this situation. Poverty led to risky situations in which girls were left unprotected from male attention. For them, it was often an utterly miserable existence in which intimate physical contact was possibly the only joy left in life that was free.

Conversely, some sections of society were open about their sexual habits and made no effort to hide it. In the bustling ports of Victorian Britain there lived sailors' 'wives'; women who lived with a man as his wife when he was on leave, but never married. They might have been the mother of the sailor's illegitimate children, or simply his intimate companion when he was ashore. They sometimes had more than one 'husband'; a pragmatic approach to the lonely life of a traveller's partner (and presumably one arranged on some form of shift system, to avoid more than one husband being in port at any one time). These relationships were often formalised to the point of a percentage of the man's wage being paid to their 'wife' while he was at sea. Whether they had just one husband, or more, these women did nothing to hide their unusual living arrangements. In fact, they appear to have often been accepted into local society with few qualms, pragmatism being a great leveler.

Edith 'Biddy' Lanchester was the fifth child of successful architect, Henry Jones Lanchester and his wife, Octavia. Brought up by her parents in Hove, Sussex, along with her siblings, Edith attended the Birkbeck Institute in London, followed by a time at the Maria Grey College,

Britain's first teacher training college for women, then situated in Fitzroy Square in Fitzrovia. After a period of teaching, Edith took up a post as a clerk-secretary in the City of London.

A dedicated socialist and member of the Social Democratic Foundation (Britain's first formally organised socialist political party), Edith was never likely to fit in with the standards required to please her bourgeois parents. But she took her rebellion a step further than anyone might have expected when she announced that, not only had she fallen in love with a working-class Irishman – fellow SDF member Shamus 'James' Sullivan – she was also intending to live with him without first getting married. Described as a 'free love union', they planned to begin these unorthodox arrangements on 28 October 1895.

Edith's father was apoplectic at his daughter's public show of outright immorality, as he saw it. He promptly hired mental health specialist George Blandford and the two men, along with three of Edith's brothers, presented themselves at her lodgings on the evening before her non-marriage was due to begin. When Edith refused to give in to the men's arguments against her union, her father handcuffed her, later justifying his actions by saying he believed her plans to be an act of 'social suicide'. Henry had planned ahead and had already filled out an 'Urgency Order' – the equivalent to applying for a section today – in order to speed things along. Blandford promptly pronounced Edith insane on the rather tenuous grounds of 'over-education'. The furious – and presumably terrified – woman was dragged outside to a waiting horse and carriage. Despite smashing one of the carriage's windows in her struggles to get free, Edith was taken to The Priory Hospital, Roehampton (now a renowned private mental health hospital and already well established as a psychiatric asylum in the late 1800s).

The *South London Press* reported, on Saturday, 2 November 1895: 'It may be stated here that Dr Blandford, who signed the certificate for Miss Lanchester's removal, and her father have both declared that they acted on the bona-fide belief that Miss Lanchester's studies and surroundings had unhinged her mind. They thought that her removal was necessary to prevent a warped and – perhaps only temporarily – deranged intellect being taken advantage of.'

The case rapidly gained public notoriety, with even the highest in the land taking an interest in the young lovers' case. The Marquess of Queensberry wrote an open letter to James Sullivan in *The Standard*, putting a case forward for going through with a marriage for appearances sake, regardless of whether the couple believed in it. From Queensberry's letter, reproduced in the same edition of *South London Press*: 'were I in your position I should go through with the ceremony of marriage, and the instant it was concluded, protest against and repudiate it, saying it was naught to you […] You have a chance now of making a public protest, as every one's attention is attracted. What is their idiotic ceremony? But it gives your wife and future children protection, and by making a public protest you and your wife clear your own consciences and are free before God and man.'

John Burns, MP for Battersea, intervened in the case, as did Edith's landlady, Mrs Grey, herself a prominent member of the SDF. Four days into her incarceration Edith was released, having been interviewed by the commissioners of lunacy and found 'perfectly sane but foolish'. After leaving The Priory, Edith never saw her father again. She immediately set up home with James Sullivan, as originally planned, and the couple went on to have two children (their daughter Elsa later became famous for playing the title role in the Hollywood classic *The Bride of Frankenstein*). Edith and James happily cohabited until his death in 1945.

The Magdalene laundries were named after possibly the most renowned Biblical figure after Jesus. Mary Magdalene is historically portrayed as the reformed prostitute, or 'sinful woman', who washed Jesus' feet with her tears.

> Her sins, which are many, are forgiven; for she loved much: but to whom little is forgiven, the same loveth little. And he said unto her, Thy sins are forgiven.
>
> (Luke 7:36-50)

The Biblical Mary might well be held up as an example of the reformed woman, but what were originally known as Magdalene asylums are now a byword for religion-based abuse of women and children; and with good reason. In 1993 property developers discovered a mass grave in an area of land they had purchased from the Sisters of Our Lady of Charity convent in High Park, Dublin. The Sisters requested permission to exhume and rebury 133 bodies, but the numbers didn't add up. The remains of 155 women were eventually exhumed from the single mass plot, victims of the harsh treatment meted out by the nuns who had run the institution with iron fists.

Women who somehow survived their time in such places found their voices were finally being heard. They told of having their names changed on admittance to the institutions, being forced to live like slaves, and working endless hours doing the laundry of the nearby towns. Many of these women would have been unwittingly washing the clothes of their own family; the very people responsible for their incarceration.

Magdalene asylums had existed across Britain since 1758, when the Magdalen Hospital for the Reception of Penitent Prostitutes opened in London. It is estimated that there were more than 300 Magdalen institutions (the final 'e' appeared later) across England by the end of the 1800s.They took in women who had become pregnant outside marriage, were considered to be promiscuous, or whose (male) family members simply considered them to be showing inappropriate behaviour. Some had grown up in the 'industrial schools' and were simply transferred to the asylums when they came of age.

These institutions became known as the 'Laundries' because many operated commercial laundry services that were staffed by the inmates. It wasn't long before financial interests took over from the responsibility of rehabilitating the women brought into the laundries' supposed care. It paid – literally – to have a ready supply of workers, so it was rarely in the interest of the management to worry too much about whether a woman really deserved to be in there or not, so long as she could work. In a strongly patriarchal society, Magdalene Asylums were a powerful tool against women who tried to buck the system.

Sometimes described as 'mother and baby homes', the laundries could essentially keep women – and their children – prisoners for years, despite them having committed no crime in the eyes of the law. Straying from the accepted societal norm was crime enough and it was a dangerous time to be a woman who didn't want to live by the rules.

The mainland asylums slowly closed over the course of the twentieth century, as modern working practices meant the laundries were no longer viable businesses. Only Ireland clung on to the old ways, with the last Magdalene Laundry finally closing its doors on 25 September 1996, three years after the discovery of the mass grave in High Park. The site has long been exhumed and filled in. Now the area is a small, purpose-built estate of smart family houses.

All this talk of virginity and purity is notable for one thing; the 'rules' were all being applied to women and girls. But what about cultural attitudes towards male virginity? Unsurprisingly, men and boys faced very different attitudes to those inflicted on the female of the species. Sexual desire was generally considered to be a normal condition for men and it was even considered potentially injurious to physical health to quell libidinous urges. Of course, such urges should only be indulged in certain ways; either with the intention of procreating with one's wife, or with women whose wellbeing mattered less, such as prostitutes or servants. Double standards were clearly and unashamedly at work, but it's unsurprising given the level of patriarchal power in Victorian society. Men didn't have to worry about getting pregnant. And should they have the misfortune to develop a venereal disease, it would be dealt with privately, the blame being put squarely on the woman for carrying the infection in the first place.

Chapter 3

Liberty, Fraternity, Fidelity

Marriage, Divorce and Adultery, Nineteenth-Century Style

We've established that the nineteenth century wasn't simply a sea of prim nightshirts and starched morals. But we can be forgiven for having made such assumptions, because Victorians of all social classes were expected to adhere to certain standards in public, even if they had no intention of living by them in private. If you wanted to have sex with someone then you were expected to marry them; or at least make it look as though you definitely intended to at some point in the near future.

As soon as a couple was married, their roles changed. Until the introduction of the Married Women's Property Act 1882, a new wife – and all her worldly goods – immediately, and literally, became the property of her husband. However affectionate and loving the relationship with her husband might be, she was reduced to little more than a chattel in the eyes of the law. And in the eyes of society, she was now expected to spend her time looking after both him and the babies that would inevitably follow.

Wives, as a breed, were assumed to be somehow above the animalistic urges of sex, while turning a blind eye to any dalliances in which their husband might indulge with other women. Physicians and pseudoscientists argued that male pleasure in the sexual act was an absolute requirement for procreation, but female pleasure was not. The female orgasm was, therefore, viewed by many as being superfluous (or even biologically nonexistent). Those women who dared to admit to gaining physical pleasure from sexual intimacy were often considered to be automatically promiscuous and quite possibly mentally ill.

Despite this, many Victorian women actively enjoyed their marital sex life, even if they'd have never dared admit as much outside the bedroom. In private, Victorians generally had a healthy and open-minded attitude towards sex – there were even theories that the female orgasm was necessary for conception, thus rendering it an essential part of marital intercourse. Sex was seen as a natural part of the human condition. Even royalty was in on the fun. Queen Victoria's endless diaries brim with excitement about how much she enjoyed private intimacy with her beloved Albert, who she idolised – both emotionally and physically – beyond all others (often to the detriment of her own children, who she appeared to view as a hindrance to the couple's privacy).

It's difficult to reconcile the popular modern image of a dour, drab monarch with the young Queen who wrote the following account of her wedding night: 'we both went to bed (of course in one bed); to lie by his side, and in his arms, and on his dear bosom, and be called by names of tenderness, I have never yet heard used to me before – was bliss beyond belief! Oh! This was the happiest day of my life!'

Thomas and Jane Carlyle were a less ordinary example of Victorian marriage, although they, too, kept up certain social appearances. Author Samuel Butler famously said of the highly outspoken and intellectual couple, 'It was very good of God to let Carlyle and Mrs Carlyle marry one another, and so make only two people miserable and not four.'

Jane Welsh was first introduced to the Scottish essayist Thomas Carlyle by their mutual friend, Edward Irving. Irving was a charismatic preacher who was himself in love with Jane, but already betrothed to someone else. Jane reciprocated Irving's feelings while accepting the impossibility of the situation and approached her eventual marriage to Carlyle with pragmatism, rather than wide-eyed romance.

The Carlyles had a notoriously prickly but longstanding relationship, seemingly based on resentment and co-dependence rather than mutual love and support. It is believed that their marriage went unconsummated, despite enduring for forty years until Jane's death at the age of sixty-five, the romantic energies of both husband and wife being almost permanently diverted elsewhere.

Jane became close to novelist Geraldine Jewsbury, with whom she developed a platonic yet clearly passionate long-term relationship that ended only at Jane's deathbed. Jewsbury once wrote to Jane, 'I feel towards you much more like a lover than a female friend'. For his part, Thomas developed an intimate friendship with Lady Harriet Mary Montagu, which lasted for some time, but it is commonly believed that the Carlyles remained faithful to one another in a physical sense, even if they were both somewhat lacking in emotional commitment.

This reciprocated loyalty implies that the couple cared more for each other than outward appearances perhaps suggested; this didn't, however, stop them endlessly bickering in the constant letters they sent back and forth. Between them, the Carlyles left an archive of more than 9,000 pieces of correspondence and it's this that makes them such a fascinating subject. The letters, along with Jane's intermittent personal journal, paint a picture of an intelligent, forward-thinking woman who played the part of a housewife with dutiful, resigned efficiency and a man of renowned and rather self-important intellect who, despite the opportunities available, was never – as far as one can tell – unfaithful to his wife. There is a slight caveat in that Thomas' fidelity may have been enforced rather than voluntary, as some historians believe him to have been impotent. Whatever the truth of the Carlyles' marriage, Thomas thought enough of his wife's written musings to collate them into a series of three books, published in 1883.

> You may be better without me, so far as my company goes. I make myself no illusion on that head; my company, I know, is generally worse than none; and you cannot suffer more from the fact that I do from the consciousness of it. God knows how gladly I would be sweet-tempered and cheerful-hearted, and all that sort of thing for your single sake, if my temper were not soured and my heart saddened beyond my own power to mend them.
>
> (Excerpt from a letter written by Jane Carlyle to Thomas, 23 September 1850)

> Much movement under the free sky is needful for me to keep my heart from throbbing up into my head and maddening it. They must be comfortable people who have leisure to think about going to Heaven! My most constant and pressing anxiety is to keep out of Bedlam!
>
> (From Jane Carlyle's journal, 6 November 1855)

Thomas and Jane Carlyle are interesting not simply because of who they were or what they did, but also because they recorded it so diligently, leaving us a window into the world of a difficult yet fascinating Victorian relationship.

The then-Prince of Wales, Victoria and Albert's eldest son Albert Edward – always known as 'Bertie' to his family – was never a stranger to scandal. But in 1870 he scaled new heights (or lows), even by his excessive standards, when Sir Charles Mordaunt threatened to name him as co-respondent in a divorce petition against his wife, Harriet.

Harriet Moncrieffe was some twelve years younger than Sir Charles, and undoubtedly much freer in her behaviour – and affections – than the dour baronet. The public assumption was that she married him for financial stability, but according to contemporary reports their marriage was a stable and apparently happy one. However, Harriet was in the habit of entertaining male visitors, alone, in the grand surroundings of Walton Hall, the couple's family home in Worcestershire. One of the most dramatic stories of the Mordaunts' marital issues tells of Charles returning early from a fishing trip to Norway to find the Prince of Wales already at Walton Hall. Bertie was watching Harriet with amusement as she practiced driving a carriage pulled by a pair of white ponies, a gift from the Prince's own stables. Legend has it that Charles chased Bertie off his land and then forced poor Harriet to watch as he shot the ponies in front of her.

Harriet may have got away with her extra-curricular activities, had she not had the misfortune to fall pregnant. When she gave birth to her premature daughter, Violet, in February 1869, the dates didn't add up. Harriet had become pregnant while her husband had been away on his fishing trip.

The baby had health issues, which Harriet convinced herself had been caused by a sexually transmitted disease. In her panic, she confessed to Sir Charles that she had been unfaithful, not only with Viscount Cole (who would indeed later turn out to be little Violet's biological father), but also with several other men. These included the Conservative politician Sir Frederick Johnstone and – even more shockingly – the Prince of Wales himself.

The ensuing scandal, described later by the *London Evening Standard* as 'pre-eminently sensational', both appalled and enthralled British society. While searching Harriet's belongings for further evidence of his wife's infidelity, Charles had discovered several letters from Bertie hidden in a locked writing desk. The letters didn't contain anything particularly incriminating, but it wasn't a clever move for a man who was heir to the British throne. Sir Charles sued for divorce in April 1869, with the case coming to court in early 1870. The Prince of Wales was summoned as a witness and appeared in open court for questioning, throughout which he insisted that, although he had indeed visited Lady Mordaunt while her husband was away, nothing improper had ever occurred between them.

Harriet's parents, realising the level of public embarrassment that was about to swamp their family, claimed that their daughter was, in fact, insane. What other reason could there be for a lady to make up such stories of adultery? Surely no rational woman would do such a thing. Some have theorised that Harriet was indeed persuaded to behave as if taken over by madness, in order to strengthen the argument that she had not been in a fit state to accept the divorce petition. The plan worked and the court dismissed Sir Charles' petition. However, Harriet – now considered to be officially 'mad', regardless of her true mental state – was committed to an asylum.

Her disappearance from public view was convenient for all concerned; all, of course, except Harriet herself. Regardless of her condition at the time of Violet's birth, Lady Harriet Mordaunt may very well have developed genuine mental health issues due to the callous way she was treated by the (vastly male) players in society's game. Five years after the future King Edward stood as witness, Sir Charles was granted his divorce.

Up until the mid-1800s, divorce was an expensive and difficult business, out of reach of all but those with enough money to fund a personal Act of Parliament – and the stamina to endure the ensuing discussions about their intimate lives in the House of Commons – or a protracted and costly journey through the annulment process.

The Marital Causes Act of 1857 changed all that by taking divorce procedure out of church control and bringing it under the jurisdiction of the civil courts (and in the process making adultery a civil issue, rather than a criminal offence).

The divorce rate increased a hundredfold in the year after the act was introduced, proving that there had indeed been many marriages that had only stayed the course because the battling spouses had no other option. But the process still wasn't an easy one. Typically of the time, the rules were different, depending on whether it was the husband or the wife who was bringing the suit against their unwanted spouse. It was much easier for a husband to justify his claim for divorce; he only had to prove that adultery had been committed. He was also required to name the co-respondent, thus adding to the potential public embarrassment for his erstwhile wife and her suitor. Should a woman wish to petition for a divorce, however, unless she could prove cruelty (the only accusation that was allowed as a reason on its own), she was required to prove not only adultery, but also a secondary cause, such as bigamy or desertion.

The act came into force on 1 January 1858, but it took until the early summer of that year for the first civil divorce cases to start filtering through. In mid-June, Henry Oliver Robinson petitioned for divorce from his wife, Isabella, on the grounds of her alleged adultery. Robinson had more proof than most, for Isabella had made the unusual (and perhaps reckless) decision to record her every last thought and feeling about her torrid affair in a diary. Her husband presented this written record for the court's inspection. According to Isabella's own written words, she had fallen madly and passionately in love with one Edward Lane, whom she'd first met at a party hosted by Elizabeth Drysdale in Edinburgh, where Isabella lived with Henry, her second husband. At twenty-seven, Lane was eighteen years younger than Isabella. He was also married to Drysdale's daughter, Mary.

Unhappy in her marriage to a man who – according to her diary entries – was unscrupulous when it came to helping himself to both his wife's and his stepson's inheritances, Isabella began keeping a diary in which she vented her misery and frustration. Whatever the truth about what really went on behind closed doors, Isabella Robinson was clearly a lonely woman who was in desperate need of supportive company.

She found that support in Edward Lane, who, despite the age gap and the fact that he was married, seemed to at least return Isabella's desire for friendship. But the diary that Henry Robinson presented as evidence to the divorce court painted a far more passionate picture. According to Kate Summerscale's examination of the diaries in *Mrs Robinson's Disgrace*, Isabella wrote of Edward Lane as her 'soul's idol', describing a particular meeting with him as being, 'full of such bliss that I could willingly have died not to wake out of it again'.

One would assume that such confessions would be more than enough for Henry to be granted his request for divorce, but the court viewed things rather differently. Women, they averred, did not have the necessary physical urges that would make such behaviour possible in reality. The only explanation, therefore, was that Isabella was struck by some form of romantic hysteria, which found an outlet in her overly emotional – and surely fictional – diary entries.

On the grounds that Isabella Robinson could not have been reporting the truth – because women simply did not possess the levels of carnal lust that her diaries described – Henry Robinson's request for divorce was refused.

The phrase 'the empire on which the sun never sets' was coined for the Spanish Empire during the sixteenth and seventeenth centuries, but by the time it was being used to describe the British Empire in the 1800s, the phrase was a literal one. Britain held control over so many countries around the world that the sun would always be above the horizon in one of them, no matter what time it might be in Victoria's homeland.

Social rules were very different for British subjects living in what were then known as 'the colonies'. At the peak of its political powers during the period sometimes known as 'the imperial century' (roughly 1815-1914), Britain's reach expanded across the globe. Although it had lost overall power over some countries – America had finally gained its independence in 1783, with Canada following in 1867 (Australia and New Zealand followed suit in 1901 and 1907 respectively) – Britain then took control of most of India, under what became known as the British Raj ('raj' being Hindustani for 'rule'), as well as large chunks of Africa. In addition, economic power meant that large swathes of the globe were, in effect, under British control.

Britain maintained control of India by the simple method of divide and rule. Despite outnumbering the British colonists many times over, the indigenous population was a divided society, ripe for pitting against one another in the games of political chess that enabled the British incomers to stay on top. The sheer arrogance of British rule in India is not to be underestimated, and neither is the level of social and political damage caused to an entire country in the name of Victoria's empire.

Nevertheless, many Indian citizens resigned themselves to making the best of the situation they found themselves in, by integrating with the British. Inevitably, some of that integration was of the intimate variety.

The Hindustani word *bibi* literally translates as 'miss', although its original meaning is closer to 'high-class woman'. Whatever its etymology, during the time of the Raj '*bibi*' became the accepted term for a native mistress taken by British colonialists. In the parallel universe of Britons abroad, *bibis* were accorded a level of respect and status that would have never been allowed on home turf. Many British men lived as if married to their Indian 'wives', socialising together and often fathering mixed-race children. The fate of such children was often insecure, despite many undoubtedly having caring fathers. Those with pale enough skin to pass as European would occasionally be sent back to Britain in the guise of an adopted child, but offspring who took after their mother's darker-skinned heritage would have to stay in India. However colour blind romance might be when on far-flung shores, interracial marriages were still not easily tolerated back in the home country.

This lack of public multicultural mingling doesn't mean that mixed-race relationships didn't happen. Unlike many other countries, interracial relationships and marriage have never been illegal in Britain, and when you examine immigration statistics for the nineteenth century – and the numbers of British families today who have distant but definitely non-Caucasian ancestors – one can only assume that, in reality, it was happening far more than anyone back then was ever going to admit.

Nineteenth-century Liverpool was a heaving port city that was growing by the year. The Great Famine (*An Gorta Mór* in Irish) of 1845-1849 killed approximately one million Irish citizens and forced the same amount again to emigrate in the hope of finding salvation in other countries. Although many simply used Liverpool as a staging post on their way to new lives in the Americas or Australia, enough of them stayed put after that first sea crossing that, by the middle of the century, approximately twenty-five percent of Liverpool's population was of Irish origin.

It wasn't just incomers from Ireland who settled in Liverpool. The Albert Dock opened in 1846 and was designed to keep shipping secure, its layout enabling boats to be moored within a secure closed dock, directly up against the warehouses. This made theft of valuable goods far less likely and the ease with which cargo could be loaded and unloaded halved the time it took to 'turn around' a ship and get it back out into open waters. Albert Dock (the 'Royal' wasn't added until 2018) was considered to be a huge step forward in shipping technology, particularly after it was fitted with the world's first hydraulic cranes in 1848. The growing levels of trade coming into Liverpool brought with it an increase in the amount of multicultural visitors in the form of sailors and traders from around the world, particularly the Far East. The Blue Funnel Line, founded in 1866, was one of the UK's largest shipping companies, establishing a regular trade route between Liverpool, Shanghai and Hong Kong. The inevitable influx of Chinese ship workers and traders led to the founding of the first

Chinatown in Europe, originally close to the docks, but later spreading up into the city itself. The current *paifang* arch on Nelson Street is the largest of its kind outside China, and since 1999 Liverpool has been formally twinned with Shanghai (alongside Cologne, Dublin and Rio de Janeiro, giving some indication of the city's far-flung connections).

With such a high density of foreign settlers and a long history of social tolerance, residents of Liverpool developed a level of acceptance for mixed-race marriages rarely seen elsewhere in the country at the time. Chinese workers married local women, the women welcoming the chance to live with men who had what they saw as a much stronger work ethic in comparison to the native competition.

A notable exception to British society's general disapproval of mixed-race relationships was the marriage of composer Samuel Coleridge-Taylor and Jessie Walmisley. Born in 1875 to Alice Hare Martin of Holborn, London, Coleridge-Taylor's father was Dr Daniel Peter Hughes Taylor from Sierra Leone, a member of the Royal College of Surgeons, who had practiced for a time in Croydon and returned to Africa, apparently unaware that Alice was pregnant (Taylor Senior went on to be appointed coroner of the Gambia in 1894).

Coleridge-Taylor – who described himself as Anglo-African – would later be lauded as the 'African Mahler', his creative talent undoubtedly easing his passage through late-Victorian society. His marriage to Jessie, a fellow student from the Royal College of Music, was initially opposed by her family because of his mixed-race heritage, but they eventually relented.

Best known for his composition *Hiawatha's Wedding Feast*, Coleridge-Taylor gained such respect and notoriety that he went on to meet US president, Theodore Roosevelt, at the White House in 1904, an invitation which, at the time, was almost unheard of for a person of African descent.

Reading these stories of love, heartbreak and passion across social divides, it becomes easier to see that nineteenth-century marriage (and divorce) was, in reality, not all that different to today's versions. Men and women alike fought to be with the person they loved, often coming up against familial disapproval. Affairs were (usually) conducted discreetly behind net curtains, and many couples stayed together out of necessity rather than desire. It may not be the most romantic of viewpoints, but often it's the mundane information that makes looking back at the past so very interesting.

Chapter 4

Lifting the Lid on Lust

Libido, Kinks and Sex Toys

We've established that the Victorians, far from being the buttoned-up prudes we thought they were, in reality were as interested in sex – both their own sex lives and what others were doing in theirs – as we are today in what we perceive to be a far more open society. We pride ourselves on being broadminded and open to the idea of kinks and fetishes, while also often being arrogant enough to assume that we're the first to truly accept them as normal points on the sexual scale. This theory is completely incorrect. If you can think of a kink, the chances are that others have been doing it for centuries.

But just how kinky was nineteenth-century British society? Let's start with the one sexy story that we all know and love for its sheer jaw-dropping naughtiness: that the Victorians invented the mechanical vibrator so that doctors could cure 'hysterical' female patients without them developing repetitive strain injury. We know the legend is true because we've read the newspaper articles, watched the films and seen the drawings and diagrams of rather intimidating looking devices; rugged machinery that, it was claimed, could 'invigorate the nerves and entire system'. Who wouldn't be tempted by that?

The problem with this delicious notion is that it is highly unlikely that any of it ever happened. The theory itself is fairly recent, having only been brought to public attention in *The Technology of Orgasm*, written by Rachel Maines and published in 1999. Maines herself has since gone on record as saying she was simply hypothesising; she had no evidence for her theory and was surprised that people ran with it in quite the frantic way that they did. The modern press is, if anything, even more prurient than its Victorian ancestors and Maines' idea was jumped on with gusto, rapidly becoming accepted wisdom. Even renowned author Naomi Wolf gets in on the myth in her otherwise excellent book,

Vagina – A New Biography: 'Some doctors […] even developed electrical masturbation machines to bring about female "nervous release". Many kinds of electric dildos were developed at this time, too, all advertised for euphemistic purposes.'

Sorry Naomi, but no. Take a moment to consider the facts. During the nineteenth century, medical science was still very much a patriarchal profession within which the scientific interest in female anatomy and women's 'problems' was dispassionate to say the least. Medical examinations were still, in the most part, done visually and from a distance, and often with the patient fully clothed. With this in mind, can we really stretch our imaginations far enough to believe that a doctor would instruct a female patient to lie on a couch and display her most intimate regions to him while he brought her to orgasm?

Such 'vibrating machines' certainly existed. There are numerous patents and evidence of many advertisements exhorting the reader to try such things as 'vibrate your body and make it well' (this from an advert for the White Cross Electric Vibrator, which rather excitingly, apparently came with a free vibrating chair). One of the best known of these contraptions was 'Dr Macaura's Pulsocon'. Later to be renamed 'Dr Macaura's Blood Circulator', the device resembled a rather cumbersome hand-cranked egg whisk, complete with interchangeable rubberised heads.

The Pulsacon is quite possibly the least sexy tool you could ever hope to see (or not) and is highly unlikely to have been used to stimulate any intimate areas. Rubbery spikes attached to a crank and spinning at high speed are an improbable method of achieving sexual relief; if anything, most people would run a mile at the thought of such a thing approaching any tender part of their body. It is immediately apparent that its more likely use was as an innocent – and decidedly external – massage for aching muscles.

There is also the danger of viewing objects from different eras within the context of our own culture, rather than against the social backdrop in which they'd have actually existed. If you do an internet search for 'Victorian sex toys', one of the most common results – usually from American newspapers of the time – is for 'rectal dilators', which look suspiciously similar to what we today would call butt plugs. The fact that they are most often shown in sets of different sizes reinforces the idea (it makes them appear similar to modern collections that are sold to those who wish to gradually develop their anal fun). However, these were actually intended to help in severe cases of constipation and haemorrhoids. The same went for the 'Rectorotor', a worryingly large plug complete with lubrication vents, which allegedly cured piles, constipation and the euphemistically titled 'prostate trouble'. The advert for this reassured potential purchasers that it was 'Large Enough to be Efficient, Small Enough for Anyone Over 15 Years Old'.

On the basic principle of 'if you can think of it, someone else has already tried it', these devices were almost certainly used at least occasionally for sexual excitement; but that was definitely not their intended purpose.

Dildos, however, were as popular as they'd ever been. A favourite private companion since humans first learned to carve stone into usefully phallic shapes, dildos have never gone out of fashion. The level of ornateness may have varied over the centuries, but the humble carved phallus has always been popular.

Victorian erotic literature is crammed with references to dildos. *The Pearl* was a pornographic magazine published in London in 1879-1880 by William Lazenby. Managing eighteen issues before being shut down by the authorities for violating obscenity laws, it includes these immortal lines from the fictional diary of 'Lady Pokingham', who regaled her eager audience with tales of her adventures prior to becoming an invalid: 'Lady Bertha took me on her knee, kissing me lusciously, and handling the dildoe as if it had been alive.' There was also this cautionary tale:

THE MONKEY AND THE DILDOE
A pet monkey who had watched his mistress fill her dildoe with cream, waited a chance when she had ceased using it, being called away for a few minutes. "Now," said he, "I will have my fill of cream," so he sucked away, but unfortunately the lady had contracted syphilis, and the monkey died in convulsions. The moral of this fable is, that you should never suck dildoes.
(Both extracts from vol. #6 of *The Pearl*, December 1879)

In 2017, an interesting lot came up for auction at Matthews Auctioneers, in County Meath, Ireland. Described in the sales catalogue as an 'antique carved ivory ladies' companion in scarlet lined leather upholstered carry box with inset bevelled glass panel', Lot 475 was beautifully – and very realistically – carved from the tusk of an elephant that had been shot in 1840. Believed to have been taken to China by the original trophy hunter, the tusk was then carved into a replica phallus, complete with secret compartment in which to keep a lock of hair from the lucky recipient's absent beloved.

Stored in a contemporary wooden Irish-made box, the item was clearly owned by a very privileged woman: very few people of the time would have been able to afford such luxurious bedside companions. However, evidence of carved phallic objects exists throughout history and it is perhaps discretion rather than rarity that ensures lack of evidence when it comes to their usage during the Victorian era. When they do appear in salesrooms and the like, there is little about them that could be described as 'coy'. In their 'Gentleman's Library Sale' of 2008, Bonham's auction house of New Bond Street, London, sold a carved ivory dildo described as having 'a smiling oriental face to the withdrawn foreskin'. The perfect gift for the lady who has everything, perhaps?

George Drysdale was the second youngest son of Sir William Drysdale, a leading figure of the nineteenth-century Edinburgh establishment. Best known for his authoritative and progressive book of around 1854, *Physical, Sexual and Natural Religion* (later editions carried the better-known title, *Elements of Social Science*), Drysdale expounded the benefits of a healthy and active sex life. He also recommended the use of what we now call condoms in order to avoid sexually transmitted diseases, as well as to allow for sexual enjoyment, free of worry about potential pregnancy. Positively liberal in his attitudes towards sexuality, in a chapter titled 'Sexual Excess', Drysdale tells us: 'Chastity or sexual abstinence causes more real disease and misery in one year, I believe, in this country, than sexual excesses in a century. We must not include venereal disease among the evils of excess, as it has nothing to do with it; it depends always on infection, not on over-use of the sexual organs.'

The liberal-minded Drysdale (who was, as an aside, the brother-in-law of Edward Lane, he of the Robinson divorce case mentioned in the previous chapter, Victorian society being a tightly knit world indeed) had, however, a secret of his own: he had risen from the dead. While travelling in Austria in 1844, nineteen-year-old Drysdale reportedly fell into the

River Danube and drowned, the tragic facts of which were reported to his grief-stricken family at home in Fife. Imagine their surprise then, when George miraculously reappeared eighteen months later. He had apparently walked home from Hungary after taking time out to recover from what appears to have been some kind of nervous breakdown.

Sometime after his return, Drysdale took a medical degree and published his progressive polemic (anonymously) during his final year. So what made Drysdale return from the tomb equipped with such fervent sexual liberalism? There is some evidence that Drysdale's interest – and indeed, his initial disappearance – were caused by his concern with regards to one of life's most natural urges. In short, Drysdale was worried that he masturbated too much. This was a common concern amongst Victorians; even the future prime minister, William E. Gladstone, wrote in his diary as a young man that such self-abuse affected him as a 'plague'. He kept notes of how this plague tortured him and what he might do to ward it off, the list of solutions including 'immediate pain'.

At this point in British social culture, the human body was considered to be a closed system of energy, within which one held a finite resource of energy that was not to be lost at any cost. Ejaculation, unless it took place during intercourse intended for procreation, was therefore widely believed to be a waste of precious, God-given resources and to be avoided at all costs, however strong the temptation might be to indulge.

These days we consider masturbation to be a perfectly safe and natural human urge. But the nineteenth century was a very different – and guilt-ridden – world for those who enjoyed indulging in a bout of hand-to-gland combat. Masturbation, or 'onanism', was seen as a disease to be cured, thus avoiding the risk of weakening the body to a dangerous level.

Some physicians believing that removal of the genitals was the only surefire way of preventing unwanted personal desire. Isaac Baker-Brown, gynaecologist and former president of the Medical Society of London, believed that women could be cured of such unseemly urges by being made to undergo a clitoridectomy. An horrific option, but one that presumably had a fairly high success rate, if only because the trauma would almost certainly put the poor woman off having that area of her body touched by another person ever again. It must be noted that Baker-Brown was later expelled from the Obstetric Society of London for performing clitoridectomy procedures as a supposed cure for epilepsy

43

and 'hysteria' as well as to prevent masturbation. To add to the horror of his behaviour, he had been doing it without patients' permission.

Baker-Brown is a good example of a bad Victorian physician. Most didn't come close to that particularly scalpel-happy gynae's arrogant awfulness, but many shared his patriarchal assumption that they knew women's bodies better than women themselves did. Female bodies were there to be fetishised and made 'other', even on a medical level. It's no coincidence that Edgar Allen Poe said in an essay dated 1846, 'The death of a beautiful woman is, unquestionably, the most poetical topic in the world.' Female anatomy mannequins had, since Clemente Susini created the 'Anatomical Venus' in the late 1700s, tended towards appearing sexually wanton: their inner organs displayed in prone bodies and orgasmic expressions on their faces, apparently desperate for clever academic men to poke investigative fingers into them. Male medical students clearly couldn't be expected to medically examine even a make believe woman unless they could find her in some way sexually attractive.

But back to onanistic finger fun. Less fortunate self-obsessed Victorian ladies would perhaps be made to wear a chastity belt. These cumbersome items of metal 'underwear' certainly existed in the nineteenth century; what is less certain is just how wearable they really were. It's unlikely that such belts could have been worn for long periods, for hygiene reasons. While acknowledging the fact that the Victorians perhaps didn't have the same idea of what actually constitutes 'hygienic' as we do today, wearing metal knickers in the days before stainless steel and modern sanitary facilities had been invented sounds like a recipe for disaster.

An important part of understanding why the Victorians were so worried about the potential side effects of masturbation is to do with accepting that they believed in the 'closed system' of physical energy. This included male expenditure (orgasm, in our terms), an excess of which was believed to cause 'enfeeblement'. What we now casually refer to as a 'wet dream' or 'nocturnal emission' was better known in the 1800s as spermatorrhoea, or 'seminal weakness'. Defined as 'excessive or involuntary ejaculation', spermatorrhoea was seen as a disease and therefore taken very seriously. Being a helpfully inventive breed, the Victorians had no end of devices designed to prevent accidental night-time erections. As we all are now well aware, these are a natural and fundamental part of male life, particularly in younger years, so one can only imagine the impossible task this was in reality.

Endless gadgets were designed to 'cure' wet dreams, including many rather unnerving variations on a metal ring with spikes on the inside. Should our poor, unfortunate chap develop a stirring in his own old chap, the flesh would swell up against the sharp points, presumably giving him enough of a shock that his trouser region would deflate again fairly rapidly.

In short, even private time with one's own body was medicalised. Obviously that didn't stop people experimenting, but one has to wonder how much psychological trauma was caused by the belief that your own body was apparently letting you down in the night.

We take it for granted these days that people enjoy different variations of intimate relationships and generally pride ourselves on accepting pretty much anything. Polyamory, submission or masochism; if it's consensual, we're cool with it. So why should the Victorians have been any different? They may not have had the social freedom to live their chosen lifestyles in public in quite the way that we have today, but that doesn't mean it wasn't going on in private.

Hannah Cullwick was a Shropshire housemaid who would have undoubtedly passed unnoticed through history had it not been for her diary, which sheds unexpected light on one of the more unusual lifestyles of the Victorian era. Born in May 1833, Hannah's mother was a lady's maid and her father a master saddler, and she enjoyed a solidly rural childhood with her four siblings. This stability was shattered when Hannah was eight years old: her father suffered business losses and the young girl was forced to contribute to the family income by working in service. The family fell apart completely when both Hannah's parents died in the year she turned fourteen. The siblings had no option but to split up in an attempt to find work across the county.

In her late teens, Hannah went to work for Lady Louisa Cotes of Sherrifhales, in Shropshire. Lady Cotes then moved to London, taking her maid with her, which is where the twenty-one-year-old Hannah met Arthur Munby, in the May of 1854. Munby had an already well-established obsession with working-class women, filling endless journals with detailed notes on their varying dialects and clothing. He spotted Hannah running errands in Mayfair, her sturdy physique and lowly status attracting him immediately. She in turn saw him as a gentleman who appreciated her dedication to hard labour. Hannah left Lady Cotes's household and took work in lodging houses and other similar positions; anywhere that would allow her more freedom to see Munby.

She called him 'Massa' at all times, long before she was actually working or living with him, when she wore a leather strap on her wrist and a locking chain around her neck, to which her 'Massa' held the key. Their relationship was that of master and servant from the start and it stayed that way throughout their lives together. Hannah apparently derived pleasure from licking Munby's filthy boots clean when he came home at night, claiming she could establish where he had been from the taste (Hannah's taste for dirty boots wasn't restricted to Munby's footwear; she wasn't fussy about who'd been wearing them, so long as they were filthy).

The power play wasn't all one way; Munby enjoyed being infantilised by his sturdy partner, who would carry him around like a babe in arms, or sling him over her shoulder. He enjoyed taking photographs of her in costume. One particularly notorious image shows Hannah stripped to the waist and blackened with soot, her padlocked neck chain clearly on view.

It took Munby a long time to persuade Hannah to marry him. She was loathe to give up what independence she had and felt that subservient work was her place in life. This fitted with her lifelong dislike of those who didn't work hard for their living. She insisted that her employers give her due time off so that she could travel to visit Munby in his chambers in Fig Tree Court, in the Temple. This was made easier in 1863 by the opening of the first line of the London Underground network, which ran between Paddington (then called Bishop's Road) and Farringdon Street. Hannah's innate sense of independence is reinforced by her secrecy – her employers rarely had any real idea where their servant was going to in her free time – and her confidence in travelling alone on the world's first underground rail line across London, in order to visit her beloved 'Massa'.

Hannah appears to have taken great enjoyment in getting as filthy as possible, as this extract from her diary entry for Friday, 16 October 1863 makes abundantly clear (she was working in service at Henham Hall in Suffolk at the time):

> Clean'd away & then to bed at ten o'clock. I'd a capital chance to go up the chimney, so I lock'd up & waited till ½ past ten till the grate was cool enough & then I took the carpets up & got the tub o'water ready to wash me in. Moved

the fender & swept ashes up. Stripp'd myself quite naked & put a pair of old boots on & tied an old duster over my hair & then I got up into the chimney with a brush. There was a lot o' soot & it was soft & warm.

Before I swept I pull'd the duster over my eyes & mouth, & I sat on the beam that goes across the middle & cross'd my legs along it & I was quite safe & comfortable & out o' sight. I swept lots o' soot down & it come all over me & I sat there for ten minutes or more, & when I'd swept all round & as far as I could reach I come down, & I lay on the hearth in the soot a minute or two thinking, & I wish'd rather that Massa could see me.

Hannah was surprisingly independent for a Victorian woman of her status and insisted on continuing to be paid a wage, regardless of her relationship with Munby. This was a woman who knew what she wanted; and what Hannah wanted was both physical and sexual servitude. Despite Munby's efforts to treat her as an equal and occasionally presenting her as a 'lady companion' at social gatherings, Hannah always resisted, once saying to him, 'I hope you'll never take me out again as a lady. It makes me miserable. I feel so useless and idle.'

Hannah eventually gave in to Munby's wishes and married him in 1873, but never settled to her new role in life. She insisted on keeping her own name, continued in her role as domestic servant within the household, and their marriage was never publicised. In a move that was somewhat ahead of the times, she also insisted that their finances were kept separate and that her new husband continued to pay her a wage. Despite her efforts to keep things on the same level as before, getting married invariably changed things and Hannah wasn't happy about it. She left Munby in 1877, moved back to Shropshire, and continued in domestic service. They stayed emotionally connected, if not physically; Munby visited Hannah regularly until she died in 1909. They had been so successful at keeping their relationship a secret that Munby's family had no idea he'd ever been married until he confessed all to his brother on his deathbed in 1910.

Regardless of the difficulties created by their unique relationship, the couple clearly loved each other very deeply. This excerpt from her diary, written before she was persuaded into marriage, illustrates Hannah's devotion to her 'Massa': 'I am his slave and he is my master freely given and freely received only for love, and while I have the chains on I am sure nothing can part us and that it is the same as marriage is to other folks.'

It is a general truism that the more repressed a society appears to be on the surface, the more likely it is that forbidden fruit hides in its underskirts. Whilst the Victorian public image was one of rigidity and prudishness, behind closed doors such restrictions only led those with darker desires to hunt them out in secret.

Flagellation was a particular favourite of Victorian erotic literature and it doesn't take a huge leap of thinking to surmise that this may have been connected to the overriding belief that any sexual thoughts beyond what accepted as 'normal' were deviant and deserved to be punished. The human spirit being what it is, people often learn to associate pleasure with their pain.

As the middle and upper classes were those with the means to identify and pursue their desires, it is most often their tastes that we see illustrated in the erotic literature of the day. Boys raised in severe educational establishments with a strong belief in corporal punishment would often grow into men whose thrill-seeking involved being whipped or humiliated themselves, or conversely, taking it out on others. In the era of servant girls and street-walkers, it wasn't difficult to find potential partners for either activity; at the right price.

The Whippingham Papers (pub. Edward Avery, 1887) was a pseudonymous collection of sado-masochistic erotica written and collated by 'St George Stock' that included unsigned verses by renowned novelist and playwright Algernon Charles Swinburne. Swinburne's most notable contribution was a piece titled 'Arthur's Flogging', which goes into intimate and endless detail about the effect of the birch on a bare bottom. So overt was Swinburne's interest in vice that it was widely assumed he talked of it far more than he indulged in it. Oscar Wilde once described him dismissively as, 'a braggart in matters of vice, who had done everything he could to convince his fellow citizens of his homosexuality and bestiality without being in the slightest degree a homosexual or a bestialiser.'

Prince Albert reportedly once told his son Bertie – the future King Edward VII – 'I knew you were thoughtless and weak – but I could not think you depraved'. Bertie's debauched activities were renowned.

Grope(cunt) Lane, Shrewsbury. Photograph by Birgitta Zoutman.

The King's Head on Mardol, Shrewsbury: a favoured spot for prostitutes and potential clients alike. Photograph by Birgitta Zoutman.

Right: If only alleyways could talk. Formerly King's Head Shut (it's thought that 'shut' is a contraction of 'short cut'), the passage leads down to the riverfront. It included at least one brothel in the 1800s and was also a conveniently discreet spot for outdoor assignations. Photograph by Birgitta Zoutman.

Below: The Royal Albert Dock, Liverpool. Opened in 1846, the 'closed' dock design made it more secure than most and also enabled cargo to be loaded and unloaded direct from the warehouses onto the ships. Photograph by Alex Butler.

Above: The sheer volume of trade coming through Liverpool's docks during the nineteenth century meant that, for a time, the city was richer than London. Photograph by Alex Butler.

Left: Busy docks meant lots of sailors and plenty of convenient alleyways between the buildings that were springing up along Liverpool's waterfront. And where there were sailors and alleyways, there were always prostitutes. Photograph by Alex Butler.

Dressed in Her Best Outfit, 1858. Alice Liddell, aged approx. six years old. Photograph by Lewis Carroll. (Wikimdia Commons, CC-BY-SA-3.0).

Fanny and Stella, aka Frederick Park and Thomas Ernest Boulton, 1869. This glass plate photograph is held by Essex Records Office. (Wikimedia Commons, CC-BY-SA-3.0).

'Portrait of Hannah Cullwick dressed as a man', 1860. From the Arthur Munby collection at Trinity College Library, Cambridge. (Wikimedia Commons, CC-BY-SA-3.0).

Portrait of Hannah Cullwick dressed as a servant', undated (thought to be c.1870). From the Arthur Munby collection at Trinity College Library, Cambridge. (Wikimedia Commons, CC-BY-SA-3.0).

The Awakening Conscience, William Holman Hunt, 1853. Photograph by Tate, London, 2011. (Wikimedia Commons, CC-BY-SA-3.0).

Left: William E. Gladstone's study within Hawarden Castle, known as the Temple of Peace. The room has been kept immaculate – and virtually untouched – since Gladstone's death in 1892. Photograph by Violet Fenn (courtesy of Hawarden Castle).

Below: Gladstone's belongings and books still cover every available surface in the Temple of Peace. Photograph by Violet Fenn (courtesy of Hawarden Castle).

Hawarden Castle, Hawarden, Flintshire, Wales. Inherited via W. E. Gladstone's wife, Catherine Glynne, the castle is still the private home of the Gladstone family. Photograph by Violet Fenn (courtesy of Hawarden Castle).

Hawarden Castle, Hawarden, Flintshire, Wales. Inherited via W. E. Gladstone's wife, Catherine Glynne, the castle is still the private home of the Gladstone family. Photograph by Violet Fenn (courtesy of Hawarden Castle).

This unassuming patch of seemingly empty ground in a corner of Highgate Cemetery West holds the remains of ten women and girls, all inmates of the London Diocesan Penitentiary. Photograph by Violet Fenn.

The Rossetti tomb in Highgate Cemetery West, where Lizzie Siddal is buried alongside the family who despised her. Her husband, the artist and poet Dante Gabriel Rossetti, chose to be buried elsewhere. Photograph by Violet Fenn.

The grave of Hannah Cullwick in St Andrews Church, Shifnal, Shropshire. Her married name of Munby is on the marker stone, despite Hannah refusing to use it while she was alive. Photograph by Violet Fenn.

Composer Samuel Coleridge-Taylor, photographed by Henry John Kempsell, 1901. (Wikimedia Commons, CC-BY-SA-3.0).

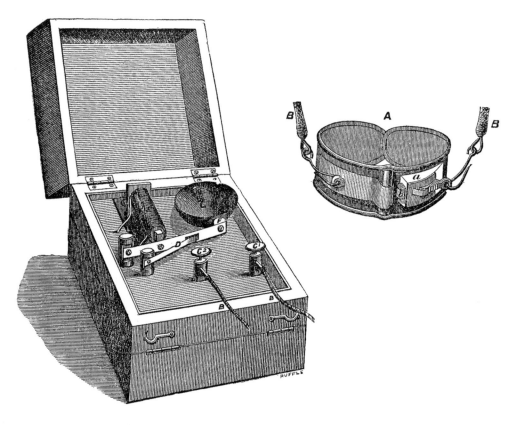

Above: J.L. Milton 'Pathology ...
Spermatorrhoea': electric alarm.
(Photograph: wellcomecollection.org).

Left: Mechanical massager,
Dr Macaura's blood circulator, made
by British Appliances Manufacturing
Co., Leeds, England, 1890-1910.
(Photograph courtesy of Science
Museum, London).

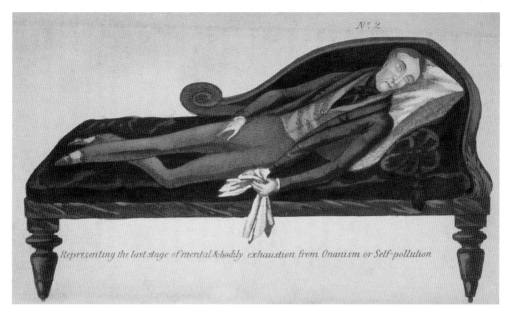

N.º 2

Representing the last stage of mental & bodily exhaustion from Onanism or Self-pollution

The Secret Companion, R.J. Brodie, London, 1845. One of a series of illustrations charting the dangers of the 'wanton waste' of semen. It was believed that masturbation could lead to a range of disorders from nervousness to paralysis. (Photograph: wellcomecollection.org).

Portrait of Queen Victoria by Franz Xaver Winterhalter, 1843. Victoria herself commissioned this rather seductive portrait, which she presented to Prince Albert on his birthday, 26 August 1843. (Wikimedia Commons, CC-BY-SA-3.0).

William Ewart Gladstone. Four times Prime Minister of Britain, Gladstone was renowned for his efforts to rescue 'fallen' women, often assisted by his wife Catherine (Wikimedia Commons, CC-BY-SA-3.0).

Alice Keppel, noted society beauty and great-grandmother of Camilla, Duchess of Cornwall. The long-term mistress of King Edward VII, Keppel even attended his coronation in 1902, sitting with the king's other favoured ladies in what was nicknamed 'the royal loose box'. (Wikimedia Commons, CC-BY-SA-3.0).

Right: Face of a woman with tuberculated ulcerations due to tertiary syphilis. (Photograph: wellcomecollection.org).

Below: Inherited Syphilis. Chromolithograph. (Photograph: wellcomecollection.org).

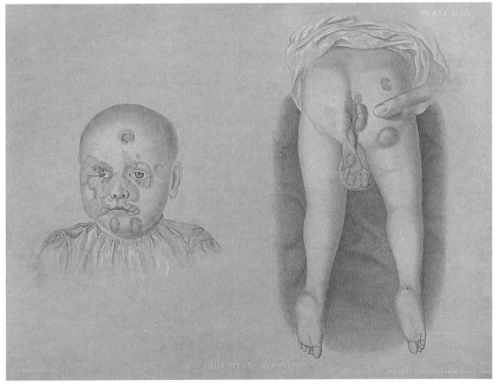

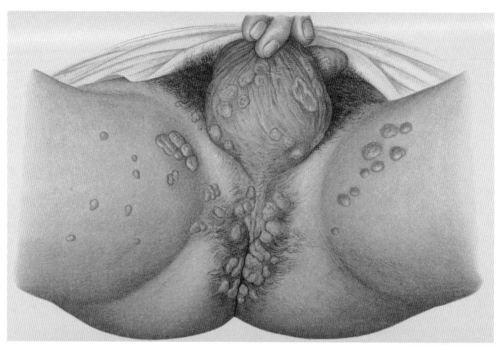

Above: Illustration of scrotum and perineum diseased with Syphilis. (Photograph: wellcomecollection.org).

Left: Ulceration of the nose, the result of congenital syphilis. (Photograph: St Bartholomew's Hospital Archives & Museum. CC-BY-3.0).

He commissioned a chair that was designed specifically for sexual encounters and installed at Le Chabanais, a famous Parisian brothel which was said to be one of Bertie's favourite haunts. Known as a *siege d'amour*, or 'love chair', it was a complicate design and anyone who has seen it could be excused for wondering how on earth it was ever used.

It's possible that Bertie saw women as objects to be conquered, making up in some way for the rather unkind treatment he often received from his mother. Queen Victoria was not subtle in voicing her feelings about things that irked her and her children perhaps felt her wrath more than most. Bertie in particular was the focus of much of his mother's frustration during his childhood. She was concerned he didn't have the intelligence needed for someone destined to rule an empire.

Just before his ninth birthday, Bertie underwent an examination by George Combe, a lawyer-turned-phrenologist who had been engaged by Prince Albert to check the quality of the royal heir's intellect. Combe's rather damning report was that the young boy's brain was 'feeble and abnormal'. Furthermore, Combe asserted, this lack of intellect was almost certainly inherited from Victoria's grandfather, King George III. As the old king had suffered from well-known mental health problems, this potential for public embarrassment concerned Bertie's parents hugely and they took steps to ensure that what there was of little Bertie's intellect was channeled in the 'right direction'. This involved dismissing his beloved tutor, Henry Birch. and replacing him with the humourless Frederick Gibbs, a destabilising move that can have only deepened Bertie's inner resentment.

The Prince of Wales' rebellion manifested itself throughout his life through endless sexual dramatics. These began with a flourish when actress Nellie Clifden was smuggled into his quarters while he was at camp with the Grenadier Guards in the Curragh, Ireland, in the summer of 1861. Brought in by Bertie's helpful friends after they had discovered that he was a sexual novice, Nellie efficiently relieved the future king of his virginity. She presumably did this with style, because Bertie's own diary records that he met with her on at least two further occasions.

The royal grapevine being what it is, word of these rather unregal activities rapidly got back to Bertie's horrified parents. Albert had been complaining of feeling unwell, but insisted on leaving his sickbed to visit Edward after the Prince's return to Cambridge University. Victoria's beloved prince consort made the trip on a cold and rainy November day,

49

and by the time he returned to London, was sickening even further. He died the next month, in December 1861. The official cause of death was typhoid, but Victoria placed the blame squarely onto Bertie's shoulders, for causing his father so much stress. She famously said of her own son, 'I never can or shall look at him without a shudder.'

When Bertie married Princess Alexandra of Denmark, in St George's Chapel, Windsor Castle, on 10 March 1863, his new wife was under no illusion that theirs would be a monogamous marriage. Alexandra had no option but to adapt to sharing her husband with his stable of fast and fancy friends, a pressure she managed to bear with (mostly) tolerant grace.

So dedicated to the carnal cause was Prince Bertie that his most favoured mistresses, both past and present, received VIP invites to his coronation in 1902. Such noted beauties as Alice Keppel, actress Lillie Langtry and Jennie Spencer-Churchill (aka Lady Randolph Churchill, the American-born mother of Winston and of whose looks it was once declared there was 'more of the panther than of the woman') watched proceedings together from a roped-off area later described by some as 'the royal loose box'.

Alice Keppel was the most established of Bertie's mistresses, her husband a willing cuckold and her family well rewarded for their royal connections. Keppel was quoted later in life as saying of the duties of a royal mistress, 'curtsey first and then jump into bed'.

It is often said that Alexandra willingly called Alice to Bertie's deathbed, but it is doubtful that the two women were quite such close friends in reality. The more likely explanation is that Bertie wanted her there and his wife could not refuse. Certainly, Bertie and Keppel were very attached to each other: Alice famously broke down in hysterics when the king finally breathed his last, having to be forcibly removed from the room by royal guards. Embarrassed by her outburst afterwards, Alice later tried to play down the event. The new King George V did not extend her any invites to the royal court after her lover's death.

And so Alice Keppel would have faded into the background of regal history, were it not for her great-granddaughter. Although there were suggestions that Bertie fathered Alice's youngest daughter, Sonia, it is far more likely that the girl was the legitimate child of Alice's husband, George. Which is probably just as well, as Sonia's own granddaughter, Camilla Parker-Bowles (née Shand), went on to become famous as the mistress – and then wife – of Prince Charles, the current Prince of Wales.

Chapter 5

Gentleman's Relish

The Rise of Commercial Pornography

Pornography in one form or another has existed since humankind started drawing rude stick figures on cave walls. The Victorians were no exception, although you'd be forgiven for being surprised at the thought as they certainly hid it away rather better than in some other eras. But however discreet they might be on the surface, there was always a seething undercurrent of illicit sexuality just waiting to be discovered; if you knew where to look.

A clever way of offering 'live' titillation without risking legal repercussions was with the *tableau vivant*, or 'living picture'. Often used as a tool for instructing an intellectual audience in the gentle art of aesthetic appreciation, *tableaux* were also used as an excuse for putting nudity on display for the paying public. As long as the models didn't move a muscle while they were being observed, it was considered acceptable.

Also known as *pose plastique*, the art form degenerated rapidly into a source of cheap thrills for the young bloods about town. One of the most notorious venues for viewing such entertainment was the Coal Hole, a tavern in Fountain Court, just off the Strand. Not to be confused with the public house of the same name that now sits at 91-92 Strand, 'our' Coal Hole was eventually renamed The Occidental Tavern, which itself disappeared when Terry's Theatre was built on the site in 1887. The widening of the Strand in 1900 finally obliterated the site entirely.

Long before Soho donned its mantle as the hub of Britain's porn industry, Holywell Street was the place to go if you were seeking illicit thrills. Situated close to what is now Aldwych in central London, Holywell – named after the 'holy well' that was fed from the River Fleet and which still exists within Australia House on the Strand – was also home to the Half Moon, the oldest shop in London. The street itself

51

(along with nearby Old Wych Street, named after via de Aldwych, now Drury Lane) was also lost to the expansion of the Strand in the early twentieth century,

Described by a writer at *The Times* newspaper as 'the most vile street in the civilised world', Holywell Street was narrow, with already-old and badly maintained buildings crammed in along either side. The jettied upper floors of the shops loomed over the casual visitor as he or she wandered the street's gloomy length. Originally populated mostly by textile traders and costumiers, the influence of many newspaper offices moving into nearby Fleet Street in the 1800s gradually changed the character of the area. Holywell Street became known as 'Bookseller's Row' because of the amount of publishers and booksellers in its midst. Approximately fifty Holywell Street premises were rather shadier than the others, hiding in plain sight by being dotted discreetly amongst the more respectable second-hand book sellers. All of these illicit traders were in the business of selling pornographic material.

One of the most notorious pedlars of porn in the Victorian era was William Dugdale, a former publisher of politically subversive pamphlets who turned to the more lucrative pornography trade after leaving his employers and going into business for himself. Initially based in Seven Dials, Dugdale eventually settled at 37 Holywell Street, where he remained for much of his working life. One of the first to be arrested under the Obscene Publications Act of 1857, Dugdale nevertheless managed to carry on his illicit trade for many years.

Unfortunately for Dugdale, the Society for the Suppression of Vice now had him in their sights. Originally founded by William Wilberforce in 1802, to enforce the 'Proclamation for the Discouragement of Vice' issued by King George III in 1787, the Society's aim was to stem what they perceived to be the rising tide of immorality within British society. And Dugdale was – in their eyes at least – a major dealer in immorality.

Dugdale's publishing catalogue included such literary gems as *Scenes in the Seraglio* and *The Ladies' Telltale*, alongside rather more down-to-earth titles such as *The Pleasing Pastime of Frigging* and *The Fanciful Extremes of Fucksters*. Incarceration was always going to be a calculated risk for someone in such a legally dubious trade. Indeed, Dugdale served at least four separate jail sentences during his working life. He eventually died in November 1868, at the age of sixty-eight, while imprisoned at Clerkenwell House of Correction.

At an inquiry into his death reported by *Lloyd's Weekly Newspaper* on 15 November 1868, Dugdale's daughter, Jessie Judge, insisted that her father hadn't been ill before entering the gaol. When pressed by the coroner as to whether she attributed her father's death to having been imprisoned, she replied, 'Yes, I attribute it to that entirely. He was deprived of books, and pen and ink and paper, and I think [it] affected his mind.'

Whatever the court's opinions of the pornography trade itself, they were clearly perturbed at the idea of an intelligent brain being deprived of culture. After returning a verdict of death by natural causes, the jury made a recommendation that 'great facilities should be afforded to the high class of men who were prisoners, so that their minds might be amused with books of a higher intellectual character than those generally distributed through the wards.'

In addition to being the inspiration for better quality prison literature, Dugdale was, during his lifetime, described by Henry Spencer Ashbee, a renowned collector of erotica, as being 'one of the most prolific publishers of filthy books'. Ashbee knew quality filth when he saw it. Best remembered for his three-part bibliography of erotica under the pseudonym 'Pisanus Fraxi', Henry was something of an authority on the pornographic art. *Index Librorum Prohibitorum: being Notes Bio- Biblio- Icono- graphical and Critical, on Curious and Uncommon Books* was privately published in 1877 and took its name from the Catholic Church's *Index Librorum Prohibitorum*, a list of books that the church believed should be banned. A second part, *Centuria Librorum Absconditorum* or *A Hundred Books that should be Hidden* (complete with the same lengthy subtitle as the first edition), was published in 1879, followed by *Catena Librorum Tacendorum/ Further Books which should not be Mentioned* in 1885. Each bibliography contains plot summaries and quotes from the books listed inside its covers.

Ashbee is also widely assumed to have been the real life person behind 'Walter', the pseudonymous author of the graphic memoir *My Secret Life*. An in-depth account of the sexual adventures of a Victorian gentleman, the author is clearly aiming for the connoisseur from the start. The frontispiece reads: 'PRIVATELY PRINTED FOR SUBSCRIBERS. 1888. This first reprint of "My Secret Life" is for private distribution among connoisseur collectors. It is strictly limited to four hundred and seventy five copies, all of which have been subscribed for prior to publication.'

Walter's recollections certainly didn't hold back on the details of his encounters: 'I spent Charlotte's third holiday with her, in a comfortable bed-room. We stopped from eleven in the morning, till nine at night, having mutton chops and ale, and being as jolly as we could be. We did nothing the whole day long, but look at each other's privates, kiss, fuck and sleep outside the bed.'

One particularly memorable anecdote told of competitive masturbation amongst a group of unnamed young men:

> At a signal, five young men (none I am sure nineteen years old) seated on chairs in the middle of the room began frigging themselves, amidst noise and laughter. The noise soon subsided, the voices grew quiet, then ceased, and was succeeded by convulsive breathing sighs and long-drawn breaths, the legs of some writhed, and stretched out, their backsides wriggled on the chairs, one suddenly stood up. Five hands were frigging as fast as they could, the prick-knobs standing out of a bright vermillion tint looking as if they must burst away from the hands which held them. Suddenly one cried "f-fi-fir-first," as some drops of gruelly fluid flew across the room, and the frigger sunk back in the chair.
>
> (*My Secret Life*, Walter, 1888.)

Perhaps surprisingly, considering the uninhibited range of subjects he happily investigated at length in his literary works, Ashbee struggled with such levels of acceptance in his own life. Becoming increasingly politically conservative as he aged, Ashbee disliked his daughters' 'excessive education', disagreed with his Jewish wife's support for the suffragist movement and became estranged from his son, Charles, for the dual crimes of being both homosexual *and* a socialist.

Another (in)famous book of the Victorian era was *The Sins of the Cities of the Plain; or, The Recollections of a Mary-Ann, with Short Essays on Sodomy and Tribadism* by Jack Saul. Published in 1881 by William Lazenby, this snappily-titled collection was one of the first exclusively homosexual books of erotica that was distributed in Britain. Containing references to many well-known characters of the time – including the cross-dressing Boulton and Park, to whom we'll return in a later chapter – the book's author took his name from a well-known rentboy called 'Dublin Jack', who was involved in several notable scandals of the era. It is unlikely, however, that it was written by the 'real' Jack Saul; more likely, it was simply inspired by his renowned sexual adventures and life as a 'Mary-Ann', a nineteenth-century term for a male prostitute.

> He rose from the breakfast-table, and opening the piano, ran his fingers over the keys; then motioning me to come to him, gave me a luscious kiss. "You darling Eveline, I'm sure your prick stands," he said, groping under my dress and finding it was as he said.
>
> "Now I will play you a nice piece, only I have a fancy to have you in me, and you must both fuck and frig me as I play to you," he said, as he made me sit on the music-stool, then raised my dress, and turning his bottom to me, lifted his own clothes and gradually sat down in my lap; as my stiff prick went up his bottom, my hands went round his waist, and I clasped that glorious cock of his, and he began to play and sing "Don't you remember sweet Alice, Ben Bolt?" from a parody in the Pearl Magazine, which he had set to music.
>
> (Excerpt from 'A Short Essay on Sodomy',
> *The Sins of the Cities of the Plain* by Jack Saul, 1881.)

Saul was clearly a writer who valued pornographic equality, for ladies were not left out of the mix: 'It is not long since we were sitting in a café in the Haymarket when a Frenchwoman of about thirty walked across the room to a young English girl and offered her ten shillings to be allowed to kiss her cunt.' (Excerpt from 'Tribadism', *The Sins of the Cities of the Plain* by Jack Saul, 1881.)

Publisher Lazenby was a very successful pornographer during the 1870s and 1880s, producing such classics as *The Romance of Lust* (1873-76) and *The Pleasures of Cruelty* (1886). Prosecuted for obscenity in both 1871 and 1881, Lazenby – along with other renowned smut-peddlers, including Edward Avery, who had produced a pirated version of *The Kama Sutra* – moved his operations to Paris, in order to continue plying his trade with fewer legal restrictions.

As with many things during the nineteenth century, pornography was often veneered with a thin layer of cultural respectability in order to transform it rather miraculously from grubby illicitness into intellectualised art. Painters have pushed the boundaries of what is publicly acceptable throughout history, but the written word is often seen as too coarse to be erotic and viewed as plain pornography, however valid and intelligent the content. That said, it is noticeable that those pornographic titles advertised as being somehow exclusive were automatically afforded a level of aesthetic acceptance by those who considered themselves to be of a higher intellectual class. Sex was always more acceptable if it could be presented as an art form, rather than mere titillation.

Photography came of age during the Victorian era. Human curiosity being what it is, where there are photographs, there are invariably models in various sensual stages of undress. The word 'photography' had only existed since 1839, when Sir John Herschel first used the word in a Royal Society lecture. As prints became easier – and therefore cheaper – to produce, interest in erotic photography expanded rapidly alongside that of more salubrious images. Though many would be considered tame by modern standards, Victorian social mores were such that a picture of a young woman in only her chemise and bloomers could be seen as the height of naughty excitement in some quarters. Photographers would occasionally feign a scientific interest in order to display the female form in graphic detail, or conversely pose them with fruit or flowers in order to lay claim to creating art rather than a cheap thrill.

As always, though, much more explicit material was available if you knew where to look, and one of the best places to look was, again, Holywell Street. Many of the bookshops had a 'special' department upstairs, for those clients who were seeking a more visual thrill. A customer in the know could have a discreet word with the proprietor, in the hope that they would be given the nod to enter the upper realm, where boxes of prints and postcards were set out for those most particular of art lovers to browse.

A brief internet search for 'Victorian erotic photography' will bring the happy viewer endless vintage images of explicit poses not much different in presentation to those one might see on the most hardcore of modern porn websites. Any lingering sense of Victorian prudishness is burned away by the endless close-ups of nineteenth-century genitals, many of them posing in a very acrobatic manner indeed. Rather amusingly, the models often have the bored half-smile so often seen on people in early photographs. Models had to hold their pose for some time while waiting for the image to 'take' as early photography was not exactly a speedy science.

These images are not restricted to individuals or heterosexual couples: there is plenty of male-on-male Victorian porn to be found, despite the legal and social restrictions of the time that surrounded homosexuality. Men can be seen *in flagrante* alone, in couples and sometimes in seething masses of taut, naked bodies, all clearly – and graphically – enjoying each other's company.

But although the cost of photography was dropping enough to bring sexy images within reach of many people, the printed word was always going to be cheaper and more easily accessible (and was more easily disguised).

The Pearl (subtitled *A Magazine of Facetiae and Voluptuous Reading*) was, as mentioned earlier, a monthly pornographic magazine published by William Lazenby in London between 1879 and 1880-81. Its very first issue contained, amongst others, the delightfully-titled essay 'Sub-Umbra, or Sport among the She-Noodles', which tells the story of nineteen-year-old Walter's visit to his cousins (the 'She-Noodles' of the title). Walter persuades cousin Annie to walk with him around the gardens and something of a sexual farce ensues:

> I could see the lips of her plump pouting cunny, deliciously feathered, with soft light down, her lovely legs, drawers, stockings, pretty boots, making a tout ensemble, which as I write and describe them cause Mr. Priapus to swell in my breeches [...] alas! a sudden shriek from Annie, her clothes dropped, all my arrangements were upset in a moment; a bull had unexpectedly appeared on the opposite side of the gate, and frightened my love by the sudden application of his cold, damp nose to her forehead. It is too much to contemplate that scene even now. (To be continued.)

Compared to modern erotic literature, *The Pearl* was relatively modest, but it was still too much for the authorities and was forced to close after a final Christmas edition in 1881.

Holywell Street became the centre of the adult industry before the concept of an adult industry was so much as a twinkle in the Soho sunlight. A century before the 'Summer of Love' of 1967, this overcrowded, grubby street, known locally as 'the backside of St Clements', was a lively and sometimes dangerous reminder that humans are, at heart, sexual animals. And animals will seek out their desires and thrills somehow, no matter how determinedly authority attempts to stamp it out.

The relatively open space of the modern-day Strand might be safer to walk down since it was widened – and it's certainly more hygienic, thanks to Bazalgette's sewerage system (installed in the area after the Great Stink of 1858 finally convinced the authorities that, just maybe, dumping raw human effluent directly into the Thames wasn't such a good idea after all) – but the spirit of fornicating London lives on in the memory of Holywell Street.

Chapter 6

One Night With Venus,
A Lifetime With Mercury

Sexual Health and Contraception

In some ways, the seemingly repressive Victorian attitude towards sexuality was pure pragmatism. Indulging in sexual contact with another person potentially carried real dangers, both social and physical. Sexually transmitted disease, pregnancy (whether wanted or not) and potential moral corruption were always lying in wait for those unwary enough to risk ignoring the warnings.

Until the development of mercury treatments in the early 1900s, syphilis was as devastating as it was insidious. And it wasn't much better after that, as the cure (which didn't always work) was often as harmful as the disease itself. Able to lie dormant in the human body for years on end, syphilis has been called 'the great imitator', as many of its individual symptoms may be characteristic of other diseases. Considering that its origin and method of contagion from one person to another wasn't fully understood in the nineteenth century, it's little wonder that people were both terrified and confused by the disease.

The signs and symptoms of the disease depend on which of the four stages the sufferer is at. Primary-stage syphilis typically presents with a single painless skin ulceration. The secondary stage brings a rash that commonly affects the palms of the hands and soles of the feet. At this point, sores may develop in the mouth and genitals. Syphilitic infection then moves to the 'latent' stage. This phase can last for years and may show no symptoms whatsoever.

At this point, a Victorian syphilis sufferer may have breathed a sigh of relief that they were finally cured, or that the genital nastiness had simply gone away of its own accord. Let us picture a typically poxed chap, who for these purposes we'll call Mr Smith. A very relieved

59

Blame and shame

Syphilis was often called 'French Disease' because the first major recorded occurrence was amongst French troops in the late 1400s. There is a tradition of blaming syphilis on countries other than one's own. The French troops had been infected while stationed in Naples, so to them it was 'Neapolitan Disease'. Others called it 'Spanish Pox', named after sailors who returned from trips to the New World with Columbus, complete with bonus infection.

Mr Smith. After all, the mercury infusions he'd suffered through must have been good for *something*. Never mind that he now had symptoms of mercury poisoning; headaches, twitching and muscle weakness were a small price to pay to be rid of the 'French disease' once and for all. And now that it had gone, Mrs Smith didn't even need to know that there had ever been a problem. After all, the doctor who had treated him was being paid to be discreet. And anyway, no real lady would want to be involved in discussion of such base topics. Better she lives in blissful ignorance.

No, he was free from worry and no one need ever know. Until – perhaps not until many years later – poor Mr Smith starts developing illusions of grandeur. He tells his wife that they have no money, because he spent it all on bow ties. But of course, they don't need money anyway: isn't his cousin that nice Mr Rockefeller over in America? He'd be more than willing to send over as much cash as the family might require, so there really is no need to worry about it all.

Mrs Smith frets and worries anyway and tries to ignore her husband while he tells her all about how the pebbles dotted on the lawn are beautiful gems and he will go out to collect them for her. As she watches him wobbling across the garden, lovingly collecting stones, she sends for the family doctor. Mr Smith is eventually admitted to the local asylum, with a diagnosis of 'General Paralysis of the Insane' (GPI). By this point he is incapable of walking without staggering and has also developed growths on his body, but these are secondary in comparison to the supervision he now needs for his irrational behaviour. Poor Mr Smith is in the end – or tertiary – stage of syphilis and won't be with us for much longer. But the connection between syphilis and GPI wouldn't be made until 1905, when research by Fritz Schaudinn and Erich Hoffmann in

Germany identified *treponema palladum* as the bacterium responsible for syphilis, and serological tests proved that many GPI patients tested positive for the disease.

And what of the soon-to-be-widowed Mrs Smith? Pregnant with their second child when her husband was admitted to the asylum, she has since given birth to a baby boy, who is doted on by his older sister. Born prematurely and a rather snuffly baby from birth, he has always been sickly but appears to be in generally reasonable health, apart from his rather strange front teeth. When they first came through, Mrs Smith noticed that they had notches in them, unlike anyone else in the family. A fun little difference, she thinks to herself, perhaps inherited from some far-back great uncle or grandmother.

Mrs Smith will not get her happy ending. Her husband will die, quite insane, in the asylum. Unbeknownst to her, her darling baby boy was born with congenital syphilis, which he caught *in utero* from his mother. It won't be long before Mrs Smith herself begins to act strangely, leaving the burden of family care to her young daughter. The poor girl will, of course, develop syphilis herself from being in such close proximity to her snotty, disease-ridden little brother. If she's lucky, she'll recover enough to believe herself cured and go on to pass it to her own children in the future.

And so the wheel of disease kept turning, fuelled by both ignorance and social standards. As men were usually the ones holding the purse-strings, it was they who were most likely to see a doctor when the unpleasant symptoms began to make their presence felt. Because of patient confidentiality – and also because private doctors knew not to upset the person paying the bills – a gentleman would very often carry on as normal with his wife, having sex and hoping for the best, because risking her health was better – to his mind – than risking his reputation.

Of course, if anyone *were* to discover his secret, he could blame one of the prostitutes he'd visited. Only on rare occasions, obviously, and it wasn't his fault if they were dirty and carried unmentionable diseases. In fact, he thoroughly supported the idea of forcing such women into having regular medical examinations, in order that real ladies such as his own dear wife wouldn't have to deal with such things.

Prostitutes were blamed for a lot of things in the nineteenth century, but particularly the spread of venereal disease. Polite society didn't want to consider the idea that perhaps the men who were paying for sex with these women might have anything to do with it. It was the women who were to blame, regardless of the fact that any STDs they carried must have come from another person in the first place. In fact, such was society's eager willingness to foist the blame for sexually transmitted disease onto anyone lower than themselves, 'fallen women' rapidly came to be perceived as the major threat, interchangeable with the disease itself. Although the phrase *femme fatale* – literally, 'killer woman' – had been around for centuries, its popularity in art and literature increased during the nineteenth century and is thought by some to be symbolic of the cultural associations between female promiscuity and the spread of sexually transmitted disease.

Syphilis wasn't the only thing that might make you itchy in the pants department, should you indulge in a little illicit nineteenth-century fun. Gonorrhoea – often known as 'the clap' – can infect the throat, rectum, and even cause conjunctivitis in eyes, as well as a burning sensation on urination and smelly, sometimes green, discharge from the genitals. Left untreated – as many cases would have been in the nineteenth century – it often causes infertility.

Even today, gonorrhoea is one of the more common sexually transmitted diseases in the UK, but it can be treated quickly and easily with antibiotics. Our Victorian friends weren't so lucky. Early treatments included syringing mercury down the shaft of the penis; an idea that had obviously been around for a long time, as a mercury syringe believed to be used for exactly that purpose was found in the wreck of the Tudor warship *Mary Rose*, which was sunk in 1545. The mercury 'cure' had been replaced with silver nitrate by the 1900s, which was in turn superseded by the development of Protargol – a form of antiseptic colloidal silver – by German commercial pharmacists.

A more unusual treatment was with 'cubeb', the small, berry-like seed of a plant of the pepper family, which today is often used as a botanical ingredient to flavour gin. Dried and ground like pepper, cubeb worked as an antiseptic and diuretic. Another popular plant-based treatment was copaiba balsam, which could be taken as capsules as well as being injected into the urethra.

Having a baby was a risky business for the Victorians, but not one that many could avoid. Lack of reliable contraception meant that those who did have sex lived with the constant risk of pregnancy. Families were large, which was just as well. Overall infant mortality rates, having declined during the late 1700s and early 1800s, began to creep up again, alongside the increasing population levels in areas of heavy industrialisation. Stoke-on-Trent – the 'Potteries' – had an infant mortality rate of approximately 200 per 1000 births in 1855, but it had risen to a peak of 225 by 1872. In comparison, the average for England and Wales as a whole in 1872 was around 155.

Few could access or afford the kind of healthy lifestyle that enables modern women – in the developed world, at least – to be reasonably confidant of surviving pregnancy relatively unscathed, and with a healthy baby to show for it. Victorians were taking a gamble against statistics when it came to neonatal health.

Living conditions were often squalid, even amongst those who were financially more secure. And hygiene wasn't given the same consideration as it is today, meaning that death during and after childbirth was a real risk for the expectant mother, despite the warnings of a few forward-thinking physicians.

Aberdeen surgeon Alexander Gordon had, through close inspection of records of medical visits to birthing or postnatal women, realised as early as 1795 that childbed (puerperal) fever was being carried from woman to woman by the medic in attendance at their baby's birth. Worse still, he realised that, in many cases, he himself was the carrier: "I could venture to foretell what women would be affected with the disease, upon hearing by what midwife they were to be delivered […] it is a disagreeable declaration for me to mention, that I myself was the means of carrying the infection to a great number of women." (From *A Treatise on the Epidemic Puerperal Fever of Aberdeen*, Alexander Gordon M.D., 1795.)

Ignaz Semmelweiz made a similar case for antiseptic procedures during childbirth in 1847, having realised the same connection between unwashed helping hands during childbirth and potential infection in new mothers. Unfortunately, for British mothers-to-be Semmelweiz was not only based in Vienna, but his beliefs went against the accepted doctrine of the day and he was widely ignored. It would be another two decades before Joseph Lister introduced the idea of carbolic acid as an antiseptic, eventually becoming known as 'the father of modern surgery". In the meantime, the women of Britain had to take their chances.

Death from complications after childbirth was so common in the mid-nineteenth century that it was seen as an almost unavoidable risk;

unsurprising in an era when doctors would swap their clean clothes for old, grubby ones on the way *in* to surgery, rather than the other way around. A pregnant woman simply had to live in nervous hope that she could give birth without tearing – the open wounds giving an increased opportunity for bacterial infection to set in – or haemorrhaging and dying from loss of blood. However natural a process childbirth may have been in theory, anyone going through it faced the very real prospect of dying, regardless of how healthy they were in general.

In the poorer, industrialised areas of Britain, rickets was common amongst those who didn't get enough vitamins in their diet and also didn't see enough sunlight. Characterised by soft and weak bone growth in childhood, rickets causes skeletal defects which can affect the spine and cause a weak and restricted pelvis. In the days before antenatal scanning, this was something that might only become apparent when a woman went into labour, only for the baby to get stuck in the deformed pelvic opening, a process we now know as 'labour dystocia'.

Today, the answer would be a caesarian section; a swift and relatively safe solution which in Britain is now commonplace for all manner of reasons. But things weren't so simple in the 1800s. One of the first 'successful' caesarians – i.e. in which the mother and baby both survived – had been carried out in Cape Town, South Africa, in 1826, by military surgeon James Barry (to add to Barry's notoriety, it was discovered upon his death that he had actually been genetically female all along, having being born Margaret Ann Bulkley in approximately 1789). But lack of knowledge about hygiene and healing processes meant that surgical intervention in childbirth was still a last ditch option to be feared. There was the possibility of a forceps delivery with the increased risk to the mother of internal tearing; not an appealing option.

In extreme cases, the only way to avoid maternal death would be 'foetal destruction'. This barbaric practice was one in which the baby was killed by using a basiotribe – an instrument that crushed the infant's tiny head – and then removed from the mother, piece by piece, out through the vagina. It is unclear, in reality, how often this process took place, as the equipment itself was cumbersome and impractical. Nevertheless, a choice between dying horribly along with the child trapped in your womb, or dying horribly from infection after the child in your womb was killed and pulled to pieces wasn't a pleasant one, to say the least. One can only assume that the majority of women had no idea of the risks in advance, or more nineteenth-century relationships might have found themselves sexless.

Unsurprisingly, most sexually active Victorians would have preferred to not develop oozing urethras and would also liked to have had some say over when – and with whom – they procreated. Contraception was a dirty word in nineteenth-century Britain, but it did exist; after a fashion.

The only realistic way of being absolutely certain of avoiding pregnancy or sexually transmitted disease before the late 1800s was to abstain completely. One can only assume that this did nothing for marital harmony between those who desired physical intimacy but didn't dare risk indulgence.

Not only was abstinence the one foolproof method of contraception at the time, it was also the only one that was acceptable across most of what was still a very religious country. Any sexual activity that wasn't undertaken specifically in the hope of procreation was considered to be against God's will. There must have been an awful lot of inadvertent sinners in the nineteenth century.

In 1877, Annie Besant and Charles Bradlaugh were prosecuted in London for publishing *Fruits of Philosophy, or the Private Companion of Young Married People,* a guide to conception and contraception that had been written in 1832 by an American doctor called Charles Knowlton. Despite losing their case – though their sentences were later overturned on appeal, on technical grounds – Besant and Bradlaugh had succeeded in bringing the topic of contraception firmly into the public eye, not least because the publicity from the trial led to them selling 125,000 copies of *Fruits of Philosophy* in the short time between their arrest and the eventual trial.

Knowlton's work was a major step forward for bodily autonomy, even if his suggestions were perhaps not the most effective at actually preventing conception. His favoured method of contraception was to wash the vagina out with a chemical solution immediately after intercourse.

> It consists in syringing the vagina immediately after connection with a solution of sulphate of zinc, of alum, pearl-ash, or any salt that acts chemically on the semen, and at the same time produces no unfavorable effect on the female.

[…] A female syringe, which will be required in the use of the check, may be had at the shop of an apothecary for a shilling or less. If preferred, the semen may be dislodged as far as it can be, by syringing with simple water, after which some of the solution is to be injected, to destroy the fecundating property of what may remain lodged between the ridges of the vagina, etc.

(Charles Knowlton, *Fruits of Philosophy*, 1832.)

Despite his clearly advanced knowledge of the reproductive system in comparison to many others of his time, Knowlton still managed to fall for some of the oldest of old wives' tales. Not only was he very doubtful that any woman would get pregnant the first time she had sex, he also believed that too much sex could in itself render a woman infertile: "Public women rarely conceive, owing probably to a weakened state of the genital system, induced by too frequent and promiscuous intercourse." He does at least make it clear that the woman could get pregnant without penetration, if semen were to come into contact with her genitals (although he thought it was because the little wrigglers might be absorbed through external membranes).

Condoms had been in use in some form or another since at least the fifteenth century and possibly earlier. After the French military syphilis outbreak of 1495 the marvellously monikered Italian anatomist, Gabriele Falloppio (after whom female fallopian tubes are named) wrote *De Morbo Gallico* ('The French Disease'), which was published in 1564, two years after his death.

In it, Falloppia claimed to have invented a linen sheath which covered just the glans of the penis and was tied on with a ribbon. His intention was purely to avoid the spread of syphilis; the earliest recorded use of any kind of sheath being used as a form of birth control isn't until 1605, when such activities were condemned as immoral by the Jesuit theologian Leonardus Lessius. The first recorded reference to anything we'd recognise today came in 1666, when the English Birth Rate Commission attributed a downward trend in fertility rates to the use of 'condons' (although one has to wonder whether the population were simply too preoccupied with not dying of plague to bother procreating).

If you look up the history of the word 'condom', the most popular story – in the UK at least – is that they were invented by 'Earl Condom' in response to a request from his monarch, King Charles II, who needed something to protect the overactive royal peenie from contracting syphilis. Disappointingly, no record has ever been found to prove that said Earl ever existed. It is far more likely that the etymology of the word comes from the Latin *'condon'*, meaning 'receptacle'. Modern dictionaries invariably list the word's origins as unknown.

As public awareness increased, so did the concern of officialdom. Parliament argued for banning condoms entirely on the principle that they encouraged unsafe sex and promiscuity; a warped logic that is too often still rolled out to this day. But progress waits for no man (or Member of Parliament) and the carnally active public were not going to give up on this sexy new invention.

In the first half of the nineteenth century, contraceptive sheaths were commonly made from animal intestine and known as 'skins'. Though available if you knew where to look, they were still too expensive for anyone other than the middle or upper classes. Advertisements for condoms began to appear in British newspapers during the 1840s, but prophylactics didn't resemble their modern design until after the Goodyear company patented a method of vulcanisation (treating rubber with chemicals to make it more durable) in 1844. Early rubber condoms began to appear by 1855 and were reusable, which made them more cost effective despite their initial higher price. They were, however, still completely out of the reach of a street prostitute: a single, reusable condom was not only more unhygienic, if it was being worn by many different clients (it's unlikely that they'd have always been washed out in between), it could cost a streetwalker the equivalent of several weeks' earnings. Another downside of rubber was that it was a heavier material than the earlier skin versions and, therefore, struggled to gain popularity because of the perceived loss of sensation. Nevertheless, the term 'rubber' rapidly became a generic name for the contraceptive sheath.

Early rubber condoms were made to a gentleman's specific intimate measurements and had to be fitted by a doctor. Manufacturers soon realised that this wasn't a practical method and rapidly developed the 'one size fits all', full-length condom. By the 1870s, E. Lambert and Son had set up business in Dalston, then a suburban village on the outskirts of London. Useable and practical contraception was finally on its way.

Chapter 7

Dark Desires

Prostitution, Philanthropy and Murder

Highgate Cemetery is spread across two separate sites on Highgate Hill in north London. The east side of the cemetery is open to the public every day and is the section that most people recognise, mainly due to the huge monolith marking the grave of Karl Marx. But if you cross Swains Lane and head through the imposing gates on the other side of the road, Highgate West is a more private place. Viewable by guided tour only, the west side is more intimate and awe-inspiring than its partner across the road, containing steep, winding paths, crumbling mausoleums and monuments whose marble finish has long been lost to the tree sap that constantly falls from the greenery overhead. Home to an impressive array of the great and the good, Highgate West is full to bursting with crooked gravestones and family tombs built almost on top of each other.

Just past the spot where legendary scientist Michael Faraday lies underneath the large memorial stone that he didn't ever want (his grieving wife insisted on installing it to remind people of his greatness), there is a small patch of empty ground. Noticeable in the otherwise crowded melee of gravestones, ivy has grown across the earth, filling the little gap with greenery. Easily mistaken as an intentional space in the burials – perhaps for drainage to come through, or maybe someone has bought the plot for future use – it comes as something of a shock when you discover that this small patch of unmarked and unremarkable earth contains the bodies of ten women and girls between twelve and forty years of age.

Purchased in 1862 by the London Diocesan Penitentiary – also known as Highgate Penitentiary or House of Mercy – the plot was used as a mass grave for those who died in the charity's care, with the last burial – that of twenty-nine-year-old Agnes Ellis – taking place in 1909. Such graves could be up to 20ft deep, the occupants interred in either a plain shroud or a very thin and basic coffin. This was for practical reasons, as much as financial; such meagre coverings would break down and rot quickly, making space for more bodies.

The first occupant of the LDP grave was also the youngest. Twelve-year-old Emma Jones died in 1862 while resident at the penitentiary, which had been established at Park House in North Hill, Highgate, in 1856. Founded to rehabilitate 'fallen women' – i.e. prostitutes – the penitentiary had a reasonably high success rate in comparison to many other workhouse-like institutions of the time. Inmates were taught domestic skills to a level that made them a very attractive prospect to wealthy local households and many had successful lives in service after their two-year stay at the penitentiary ended. Poet Christina Rossetti volunteered at the establishment for more than a decade and would have been there while Emma was in residence.

Born in Sawbridgeworth, Herfordshire, young Emma Jones travelled the twenty-five miles to the Hornsey area in approximately 1859, when she was a mere ten years old. It can't have taken long for the little girl to fall foul of the many dangers of the big, bad city, because she was listed as an inmate at the penitentiary by the time of the 1861 census. Tour guides at the cemetery talk kindly and sympathetically about the fate of such a young child and those alongside her in the unmarked grave.

But was Emma Jones really only twelve when she died, or could the truth be rather more convoluted than that? According to the census return that lists her as being a resident of the penitentiary in 1861, Emma was born in Sawbridgeworth in 1849, a date that backs up the claims of her extreme youth. It is worth remembering, however, that it would have been Emma herself giving her details – whether that was for the census itself or for the penitentiary records when she was first admitted – and there is no way of knowing whether the information she gave was correct.

Official records show that there was an Emma Jones resident in Sawbridgeworth in 1851, the seven-year-old daughter of Edward and Sarah Jones. A matching entry in the Christening Index gives Emma's birthdate as 25 March, 1844. There are no other records that fit, and these dates would suggest that 'our' Emma was actually around eighteen years old when she died. She was still tragically young, but possibly a young adult rather than a child. Might she have lied, and if so, why?

Assuming that Emma was naturally small and looked younger than her real age, it's possible that she used this to make her case for admission to the penitentiary more likely to succeed. By giving her year of birth as 1849, she would have presented to the admissions board as a ten-year-old desperately in need of assistance, rather than a fifteen-year-old, who, in the late nineteenth century, would have been considered an adult and possibly a less sympathetic case.

There is also the grim possibility that Emma had been implying she was much younger than she really was in order to attract a depressingly familiar type of client; one who prefers the attentions of a child above those of an adult. In a world where the only thing earning money was her body, it wouldn't take long for a young girl to realise that she could potentially play on her image in order to attract more business. With few surviving records – and even those written by potentially unreliable witnesses – there is no way of knowing for sure how old Emma Jones really was, or what led her to a lifestyle that ended in an anonymous mass grave in a cold corner of north London.

Eliza Armstrong was another girl who experienced far too much at too young an age, but in her case, her trauma was created for the express purpose of selling newspapers. William Thomas Stead was the editor of *The Pall Mall Gazette*, a London evening newspaper which was eventually absorbed into the *Evening Standard*. At the time of Stead's leadership, the *Gazette* was a Liberal-leaning paper with designs on becoming a leading investigative publication. Concerned by tales of child prostitution in the city – and with an eye on attracting more readers – Stead made arrangements to procure a young girl as proof that such immoral purchases were, indeed, possible. The resulting coverage was, in effect, the foundation stone for New Journalism, in which the media puts itself in a position of power and forces governmental action based on its own investigations and political machinations.

Convincing reformed brothel-keeper Rebecca Jarrett to help with his project, Stead persuaded her to use old contacts from her days as a prostitute to procure a young girl for him, which she duly did. Elizabeth Armstrong was an alcoholic, and she needed the money that Jarrett offered. She agreed to sell her daughter, Eliza, for five pounds, although she would later insist that she believed her daughter to be going to work as a housemaid. The girl was first examined by a midwife in order to prove she was a virgin, then taken to a brothel and drugged with chloroform. Left alone to await her 'purchaser', Eliza awoke and screamed when she saw Stead in the room. He left, satisfied that the girl's audible fear would imply that he had taken full advantage of the situation. Eliza was then taken to France with the help of Bramwell Booth, (whose father William had founded the Salvation Army), and was left in the care of a Salvationist family.

Titling their crusade 'The Maiden Tribute of Modern Babylon', the *Gazette* threw everything into creating what we would now recognise as classic sensationalist tabloid journalism. Stead gave a dire warning to his readership ahead of publication: 'All those who are squeamish, and all those who are prudish, and all those who would prefer to live in a fool's paradise of imaginary innocence and purity, selfishly oblivious to the horrible realities which torment those whose lives are passed in the London inferno, will do well not to read the Pall Mall Gazette of Monday and the three following days.'

This immediately made the *Gazette* the evening read of choice, paving the way for tabloid journalism the world over. The articles themselves were designed to titillate as much as possible, with headers such as 'The Violation of Virgins' and 'Confessions of a Brothel-Keeper'. In the section 'A Child of Thirteen Bought for £5' Stead relayed Eliza's story, changing her name and omitting to mention that he himself had arranged the entire transaction for the purposes of the investigation.

W.H. Smith, the main news vendors of the time, refused to carry the newspaper due to what it considered to be inappropriate content. The *Pall Mall Gazette* was instead sold to the eager public via street vendors and Salvation Army volunteers; even second-hand copies found an enthusiastic market, selling for many times their original cover price. Stead's campaign whipped up such a fervour that the Home Secretary feared rioting on the streets and requested that he call a halt, but Stead refused to do so unless the government agreed to pass the laws he considered necessary to end the supposed child prostitution crisis. Cornered by an angry populace and a newspaper that wouldn't back down, parliament resumed debate on the Criminal Law Amendment Act (subtitled 'An Act to make further provision for the Protection of Women and Girls, the suppression of brothels, and other purposes').

Stead, however, was to pay dearly for his media success. Investigations by rival newspapers had unearthed the true story of 'Lily' and Stead's part in it. Eliza's mother went on record as saying she had certainly never given permission for her daughter to go into prostitution and Jarrett hadn't bother to seek approval from the child's father. Stead and Jarret were charged with assault and abduction, along with others connected to the case. Both were found guilty, along with the midwife who had examined Eliza; all other participants were acquitted. Despite being the mastermind behind the entire operation, Stead was sentenced to three months in prison, considerably shorter than the six months given to the two women. He was considered a 'first-class inmate', later describing his time in Holloway as a pleasant holiday.

Rudyard Kipling's 1888 short story *On The City Wall* tells the story of the beautiful Lalun, 'a member of the most ancient profession in the world.' The phrase had previously been used to describe many trades, but has been accepted as referring to prostitution ever since.

Even before Kipling gave it such a renowned soubriquet, the nineteenth century was a high water mark in the sex trade. Increased industrialisation led to overcrowded towns and cities, their populations ever-increasing as those from more rural areas were tempted to try their luck in the new modern industries. Poverty was rife, and for many women struggling to survive in a time before the welfare state, prostitution was an obvious method of survival. But it was far from being the easiest: danger lurked on every street corner, from violent punters to violent law enforcement.

The origin of the term 'red-light district' is confused and undecided. Some say it comes from early American railroad men leaving their red lamps outside brothels in order for their fellow crew members to know who to alert before the train moved off: others, meanwhile, argue that the moniker has its beginnings in the red paper lanterns often hung outside Chinese brothels to denote the type of trade being carried on inside.

Although almost all towns and cities in Victorian Britain had their share of ladies of easy virtue, Liverpool overtook them all to become what historians now sometimes describe as 'the European capital of prostitution'. With the increase in world trade coming in via the port's rapidly expanding docks, the numbers of sailors and traders seeking their fortunes increased rapidly. And where there are sailors looking for shore-based entertainment, there are always women willing to entertain them, and sometimes to fleece them of their wages.

The song 'Maggie Mae' (often credited to the Beatles, it was actually known as early as 1830 as a traditional folk song) tells the story of a Liverpool prostitute who is caught pawning the clothes of a man she's taken to her bed:

And the judge he guilty found her of robbin' a homeward-bounder, she'll never walk down Lime Street anymore.

Oh Maggie Maggie Mae, they have taken her away and she'll never walk down Lime street anymore.

Well that judge he guilty found her, for robbin' a homeward-bounder, you dirty robbin' no good Maggie Mae.

Considering the depths of poverty in which so many of the prostitutes were living, it is perhaps unsurprising that some of them did indeed steal from their customers. Living almost entirely unprotected in a society that blamed them for the spread of immorality and disease, yet also used their services with careless aplomb, the occasional theft of a wallet or watch from an unsuspecting client was perhaps seen as something of a justifiable bonus.

With widespread prostitution came widespread disease. The spread of syphilis and gonorrhoea was blamed on the prostitutes who were infected by their clients and then couldn't afford treatment, rather than on the men who used their services. The hypocrisy surrounding sex workers in the Victorian era was astounding. It was considered as acceptable, almost normal, behaviour for a man to have 'urges' that he might want to assuage by paying for sex, but at the same time, the prostitutes providing such services were considered immoral and – literally – dirty. Prostitutes were considered to be a walking health hazard that needed to be contained, rather than being people in their own right.

The various Contagious Disease Acts were passed in 1864, 1866 and 1869 and were intended to curb the spread of venereal disease, particularly amongst the military. Under the acts, the police were given powers to detain any woman suspected of prostitution, without any evidence being required to justify suspicion. Many an unfortunate woman was picked up by the plain-clothed police units who patrolled certain areas, looking for women they might bring in on suspicion of soliciting.

Regardless of whether the detained women were actually prostitutes, they would then be forced to undergo a humiliating and intrusive medical examination to check them for STDs. Any woman refusing to be examined could be imprisoned and sentenced to hard labour. Butler (see below) described these examinations as 'surgical rape' and campaigned vociferously against them.

In her paper '*Singular Iniquities: Josephine Butler and Marietta Higgs*'(New Blackfriars Journal Vol. 71, January 1990), historian Hilary Cashman suggests that because a woman's name was automatically blackened by the simple fact she'd been pulled in by the police, some had no option but to turn to prostitution after the event, as they would then be considered unsuitable for other, more respectable employment. The number of women whose lives were ruined simply as a result of unfounded suspicion or malicious gossip must have been considerable.

Those unfortunates who were found to be carrying a sexually transmitted disease were then transferred to a 'lock hospital' for set periods that were initially set at three months, but with the 1869 Act were extended to a full year. There was no process of appeal. Lock hospitals were so named after their origins as units built to house leprosy victims who were kept in restraints. Women who were moved to these depressing places were forced to undergo treatment for their condition and held there until they were deemed to be clear of disease and no longer a threat to society.

Not everyone in polite society judged those who were involved in prostitution; there were some who actively tried to help. Josephine Butler (née Grey) was the daughter of one of the cousins of former prime minister, Lord Charles Grey and once claimed by Prince Leopold, youngest son of Queen Victoria, to be 'considered by many people … the most beautiful woman in the world'. She married schoolmaster George Butler in 1852, the couple then setting up home in Oxford, where Josephine felt stifled by what she perceived as a claustrophobic and misogynistic academic community.

The Butlers' five-year-old daughter, Eva, died in 1864 after falling from banisters onto the stone hall floor of the family home. The loss of the youngest of her three children affected Josephine deeply and she developed depression. This culminated in a physical breakdown a few months after Eva's death, while she was on a recuperative trip to Naples with her middle child, Stanley, who was himself recovering from the diphtheria that he'd suffered soon after his sister's death.

The Butlers moved to the Dingle area of Liverpool in 1866, in order that George might take up a post as headmaster of Liverpool College.

The move to the north-west was a turning point for the still-traumatised Josephine. Writing her husband's biography in 1892, two years after his death, she spoke of her need to find distraction and solace within the poorer community around her. 'I only knew that my heart ached night and day, and that the only solace possible would seem to be to find other hearts which ached night and day, and with more reason than mine [...] my sole wish was to plunge into the heart of some human misery, and to say [...] "I understand. I, too, have suffered." It was not difficult to find misery in Liverpool.' (Josephine Butler, *Recollections of George Butler*)

Josephine got into the habit of visiting Brownlow Hill workhouse, where she could often be found sitting on the floor of the cellars with the female inmates, picking oakum (a painstakingly slow job that involved unraveling old ropes into individual strands) while praying and reading out passages from the Bible. It wasn't long before the Butlers began to take the most needy of the women – often those who were terminally ill with complications from sexually transmitted diseases – into their own home, but it rapidly became clear that this was simply not enough and a more permanent solution would need to be found.

In the spring of 1867 Butler opened her 'Industrial Home' on Myrtle Street in Edge Hill, funded by the workhouse committee and local merchants. The Industrial Home gave women a safe place to stay while also carrying out slightly more productive work such as mass-producing envelopes and sewing.

Josephine Butler strongly believed that women needed an education, in order to lessen the chances of them ending up back on the streets after their time in the home. In 1868 she published *The Education and Employment of Women*, in which she argued for more equal access to employment for women, as well as the right to further education. Campaigning alongside suffragist Anne Clough, Butler was also influential in the eventual decision by the University of Cambridge to introduce examinations for women in 1869.

But it was for her fight against the Contagious Diseases Acts that Butler is still best known. She clearly viewed it from the start as a form of patriarchal abuse by those in authority who wished to take control of women's autonomy and, indeed, their physical bodies. In *Personal Reminisces of a great Crusade* (1910), Butler says: 'The legislation we opposed secured the enslavement of women and the increased immorality of men; and history and experience alike teach us that these two results are never separated. Slavery and License lead to degradation, political ruin, and intellectual decay'.

Outraged by the hypocrisy and abuse that was in effect legitimised by the Contagious Diseases Acts, Butler joined essayist and suffragist Elizabeth Wolstenholme in founding the Ladies National Association for the Repeal of the Contagious Diseases Acts (LNA) in late 1869. On 1 January 1870 the LNA published an article titled 'Women's Protest' in the *London Daily News*, which included the following sharp takedowns of the Contagious Diseases Acts (edited for brevity):

> [...] it is unjust to punish the sex who are the victims of a vice, and leave unpunished the sex who are the main cause, both of the vice and its dreaded consequences [...] by such a system, the path of evil is made more easy to our sons, and to the whole of the youth of England [...] these measures are cruel to the women who come under their action – violating the feelings of those whose sense of shame is not wholly lost, and further brutalising even the most abandoned.

> [...] the disease which these Acts seek to remove has never been removed by any such legislation. The advocates of the system have utterly failed to show, by statistics or otherwise, that these regulations have [...] reclaimed the fallen, or improved the general morality of the country.
>
> Excerpts from Women's Protest

The LNA, alongside other groups of activists, eventually succeeded in getting the Contagious Diseases Acts repealed in 1886. The groundswell of opposition to the acts wasn't entirely down to Butler's work; many had joined the activists in protest at the perceived erosion of civil liberties, and particularly the violation of human rights. The repeal of these laws had the side effect of formally criminalising prostitution, as the acts themselves had made sex work legal by the very act of regulating the industry.

Regardless of legalities, Liverpool's sex workers continued on their busy way, helped by the constant influx of new customers coming into town via the ever-expanding docks. It was said that women would loiter outside the Sailors' Home in Canning Place, waiting for the men to be paid, in the hope that they might be looking for some fun activities on which to spend their money. The layout of Liverpool waterfront gave plenty of space for prostitutes to ply their trade: it's said that women were kept busy from Castle Street, all the way down through Wapping and as far south as Parliament Street.

There is a temptation to assume that prostitutes as a breed were being used by men and are therefore to be pitied, but while the streetwalkers of Victorian Liverpool certainly deserve sympathy for the overcrowded and unhealthy living conditions, and the dangerous lifestyle that they led, there was a level of independence to be had from selling one's body to the men looking for five minutes of fun in the city's alleyways. Of course, this autonomy wasn't appreciated in a patriarchal society, although some did at least recognise the double standards. As far back as 1859, in *Prostitution considered in relation to its cause and cure*, James Miller wrote of the hypocrisy surrounding an individual's potential to be accepted back into society after 'breaking the rules' and how women were invariably treated differently: 'A woman falls but once and society turns upon her as soon as the offence is known. A man falls many times, habitually, confessed by; yet society changes her countenance on him but little, if at all.'

An entire industry has built up around the brutal acts of one person that took place over the course of a few short weeks in the autumn of 1888. The extreme levels of violence involved in the attacks that became known as the 'Ripper murders' (the victims all had their throats cut, one right through to her spine), and the speed at which the attacks took place, meant that people had no choice but to take notice.

Whitechapel was just another overcrowded London slum where violence was endemic, but the newspapers were quick to pick up on the story. It could be argued that the media itself created 'Jack', whose identity has never been established. Although it is widely accepted that there are five 'official' Ripper victims – Mary Ann Nicholls, Annie Chapman, Elizabeth Stride, Catherine Eddowes and Mary Jane Kelly – there were several other murders that have been considered as part of the killing spree. Even among the accepted five, there is some argument to be had about whether they were really all murdered by the same person. Although Elizabeth Stride's throat was cut when her body was found in the early hours of Sunday, 30 September by the luckless secretary of a nearby socialist club in Berner Street (now Henriques Street), she hadn't been mutilated in the same way as the other women. Furthermore, the next victim, Catherine Eddowes, was found only forty five minutes later, almost a mile away in Mitre Square, in the City of London. The unfortunate Catherine had been the victim of the most horrific mutilation, having had her throat cut, been disemboweled and her intestines strewn over her shoulder, as well as one ear being sliced through.

It is worth pointing out here that, regardless of what endless books, essays and films claim, it is very unlikely that all of the Ripper's victims were prostitutes. Hallie Rubenhold's book *The Five – The Untold Lives of the Women Killed by Jack the Ripper* (Doubleday, 2019) is a rare attempt to give the Ripper's victims the dignity they've so long been denied. In it, she describes their real, visceral lives in affectionate detail and notes that several of the women were almost certainly not prostitutes; they were just poor. You don't even need a book to realise that it is unlikely that all of the victims of the Whitechapel murders were sex workers. A trawl of the internet will tell you that only one of the five Ripper victims – Mary Jane Kelly, the last of the five to die – was unquestionably working solely as a prostitute. But regardless of evidence – or lack thereof – all of the women were labeled as such. This view informed public opinion from then on, right up to the present day. It plays into the old and tedious trope of Madonna versus whore; the implication being that the victims somehow brought their fate upon themselves by not fitting the expected template of what society expected of a woman. One only has to look at the case of the Yorkshire Ripper to see a more modern example of this continuing bias.

The voyeuristic detachment of almost all contemporary accounts of the Whitechapel murders shows just how 'other' prostitutes were perceived to be, in comparison to the rest of society. Coming at a time of increased literacy amongst the populace, and the eagerness of newspapers to shock and titillate their readers, the myth of Jack the Ripper rapidly developed a life of its own. In a time before efficient forensic science, many clues were lost or simply ignored and the myth had freedom to grow unchecked.

Because the murders occurred during the early days of photographic evidence, images of the women's mutilated corpses now pop up whenever you search for information on the Ripper murders online. Harshly monochrome photographs of the women's naked and disfigured bodies appear everywhere, laid out for everyone to look at as though they're nothing more than slabs of meat on display in a butcher's window.

Even back in 1888 people wanted to see the gory details with their own eyes. The *Illustrated Police News* of Saturday, 8 September 1888 helpfully published an artist's impression of Mary Nicholls lying in a coffin – with her throat clearly cut – on the front and centre of the cover, surrounded by portraits of those investigating the case. Labelled 'The murdered woman, Whitechapel mortuary', Mary is used as the nineteenth century's version of clickbait while at the same time not being deemed important enough to deserve to be named. Her inert corpse is the centre of attention, but is displayed passively – almost prettily – in the centre of a frame of images depicting the presumably go-getting gentlemen who were now in charge of her. The sheer vulnerability is heartbreaking, even looking at the images from more than a century's distance.

The brutal and endlessly fascinating murders have spawned an entire industry, with many competitive 'Ripper Tours' offering to escort you on a pleasant stroll around the East London locations of so much mayhem and killing. 'Ripperologists' have turned a madman's rampage into a pseudo-science of research, investigation and endless hypotheses that focus on the psychology behind the killings while ignoring the real people at the heart of individual tragedies.

The likelihood is that 'Jack the Ripper' was, in reality, nothing more than a sad and sorry man with a twisted mind and a need to take vengeance on women, for reasons we'll never fully understand. Perhaps he killed more than the five; or maybe they weren't all victims of the same person in the first place. Many other women died in similar circumstances and didn't make the headlines. There was a third murder on the night of the 'double event' that mirrored the others almost exactly; the difference being that, in this particular case, the woman's husband admitted that he was responsible for the attack. Correlation doesn't automatically equal causation. The most unfortunate part of the story is that Jack himself was – and still is, with the exception of a very few publications, including Rubenhold's excellent book – seen as the most interesting character in the sorry tale. The women he murdered in cold blood are all too often reduced to side characters, rather than being at the cold dead heart of an evil tragedy.

Eight little whores, with no hope of Heaven,
Gladstone may save one, then there'll be seven

These macabre opening lines are from a rhyme which became popular in London at the time of the Ripper murders. While counting down the fates of the unfortunate women who died at the hands of the notorious serial killer, the unknown author also takes a sly swipe at the (then former) prime minister, William Ewart Gladstone.

Gladstone would begin his fourth stint as PM in 1892, cementing his reputation as a pillar of Victorian political society. But however deeply entrenched he might have been within the political establishment, he wasn't above concerning himself with the wellbeing of the lower classes. Gladstone developed an interest in the welfare of those women who had turned to prostitution in order to survive the harsh living conditions of the nineteenth century.

What Gladstone would later describe as his 'rescue work' began in 1840, patrolling the streets of London (as well as Brighton, Milan and Nottingham, making it something of a European tour of the sex trade) in search of women who might be thankful of his support. He would stop to speak to them in the hope of encouraging them to change their ways, often accompanying them back to their lodgings in order to discuss their situation late into the night. Sitting at his desk in the 'Temple of Peace', his study within Hawarden Castle, Flintshire, Gladstone engaged in endless correspondence with, and about, the women he so desperately tried to save.

The study has been preserved by Gladstone's descendants and has barely altered since the statesman's death in 1894. One can stand behind the great man's desk and look out across the castle grounds at the same view that Gladstone would have seen when he was busy writing his many encouraging letters of support to those he was attempting to help.

It was noted that his interest tended towards the more attractive of the damsels in distress. His Parliamentary colleague, Henry Labouchère, famously said of him, 'Gladstone manages to combine his missionary meddling with a keen appreciation of a pretty face. He has never been known to rescue any of our East End whores, nor for that matter is it easy to contemplate his rescuing any ugly woman.' One can only assume that the East End ladies of the Ripper rhymes were left to fend for themselves.

It is clear from Gladstone's own archives that there was some concern among his staff as to whether his apparent good deeds could be his undoing. There was particular concern about the risk of blackmail potentially arising from his rather unusual approach to such a politically charged social problem, and later reports show that official staff had read through some of Gladstone's correspondence in order to confirm that there was nothing of concern contained within them.

When seen in the context of the time, it seems far less likely that Gladstone's motives were morally dubious. He was possibly more inclined towards using his charitable works, at least in part, as diversionary tactics for his own libido, without necessarily having questionable intentions towards the women themselves. His wife, Catherine, was of a similar mind and almost certainly the driving force behind many of the couple's charitable works. Particularly after the couples' seven surviving children reached adulthood (the eighth, Catherine Jessy, having died before her fifth birthday), Catherine threw herself into her own good works, travelling all over the country in support of various causes.

Regardless of outside opinions, Gladstone determinedly continued his rescue work, and indeed, had some success in his endeavours. He managed to persuade several women and girls into leaving the streets in favour of either employment (where he could find it for them) or alternatively, into training as domestic servants. Catherine Gladstone is believed to have willingly taken such women into their London home when William could find no other place for them, feeding them and giving them a safe bed for the night.

The Gladstones between them developed quite a habit of taking in all manner of waifs and strays. At one point, the Hawarden Castle estate was home to not only the Gladstone family and their staff, but also several mill girls who had been retrained as domestic servants, and a group of boys who had been orphaned by the cholera epidemic. It certainly wasn't unusual or unlikely for there to be a few extra residents under the Gladstones' protection, however colourful their guests' previous lives might have been.

Gladstone himself was seen as something of an amusing figure to the subjects of his interest, who allegedly called him 'Old Glad-Eye' in private. But in the main, the women he worked with tolerated his perceived interference in return for the flattery that came with being 'rescued' by a man of such high status.

One particular woman has become notoriously enmeshed in Gladstone's story. Having started her career as a Belfast streetwalker, alongside her day job as a shop assistant, Laura Bell allegedly had an affair with William Wilde – father of Oscar – before moving to London sometime around 1849. Rapidly becoming known as 'The Queen of

London Whoredom', Laura's many talents were particularly appreciated by Jung Bahadur Rana, the Nepalese prime minister, with whom she had a brief but expensive (for him, at least) affair in 1850. Installing her in a lavish house on Wilton Crescent, Belgravia, the besotted Rana is believed to have spent around £250,000 on Bell over the ninety days they were together; a sum large enough that it required being underwritten by Lord Canning, the then-Governor-General of India.

Rana eventually tore himself away in order to return to Nepal, but even then could never refuse a request from Bell, to whom he had pledged eternal loyalty. Concerned about the plight of British troops during the Sepoy Mutiny of 1857, Bell wrote to Rana requesting his help. Rana kept his word, and in sending his own troops to assist the British, established the tradition of Gurkha soldiers serving in the British military.

In 1853 Laura Bell married Captain Augustus Thistlethwayte and moved into his home on Grosvenor Square. It was something of an unexpected pairing and the marriage is not considered to have been a happy one. However, it was certainly transformative. Soon after their marriage, the Thistlethwaytes attended a speech by evangelical preacher Richard Wagner and underwent something of a religious experience. Bell became a preacher herself, describing herself as 'God's Ambassadress' and taking on welfare work around the problem of prostitution.

The Thistlethwayte's marriage deteriorated, mostly due to Laura's spendthrift ways. Augustus paid his wife's bills for some time, but eventually grew tired of her behaviour and cut off her credit. Nevertheless, the couple stayed together until Augustus died in 1887 at the age of only fifty-seven, as a result of a rather mysterious accident. Known for his occasionally eccentric behaviour, the captain would often call his servants by shooting his pistol into the ceiling above him. While possibly reckless, this habit also implies that Captain Thistlethwayte was confident enough with a gun to be able to shoot it indoors without injuring anyone.

However, on Sunday, 7 August 1887, Thistlethwayte fell over in a faint while getting ready for bed, knocking his revolver off the bedside table as he did so and somehow managing to shoot himself in the head as he fell. Although fatal, it wasn't instantaneous. His death certificate stated, 'Pistol Shot Wound in Head Accidentally when carrying a loaded pistol found in a helpless condition on the floor and died in 14 Hours' (sic).

His untimely death certainly solved Laura's financial problems, as he left her more than £71,000 in his will (just over £9million in today's money). It's interesting that no one ever seriously questioned the somewhat suspicious circumstances of Augustus Thistlethwayte's demise, especially as several newspaper reports of the time described it rather archly as 'a singular death'.

This lack of desire to ask too many questions may have been down to Laura's network of powerful friends, the most powerful of whom was William Ewart Gladstone. Laura had become friendly with Gladstone – with whom she had charitable interests in common – soon after her religious conversion. She became closer to both William and Catherine after her husband's death, the couple staying at Bell's Grosvenor Square home when visiting London.

Gladstone wrote to Bell on a regular basis, clearly seeing her as an intellectual equal worthy of encouragement and support. Despite efforts by many historians over the years to connect the pair on a romantic level, there is no concrete evidence that theirs was anything other than a friendship based around similar professional interests, however unlikely their connection might seem to modern eyes. Perhaps they recognised a likeness in one another; a determination to do as they pleased, regardless of the opinion of others, alongside a deep-seated desire to help those who had been less fortunate. Something of the 'there but for the grace of God' argument.

Or perhaps there *was* a relationship of sorts that both Gladstone and Laura Bell skirted around for years, kept apart by circumstance yet drawn together by mutual attraction. However hard the investigative historians attempt to pry into Gladstone's private life and thoughts, no one can ever be truly sure what Laura Bell really meant to him.

Whatever his personal reasons for initially becoming involved in the rehabilitation of 'fallen women', William Ewart Gladstone persisted in doing what many of his social standing would have baulked at: he saw the women as fellow human beings, as deserving of care and respect as anyone else.

The 'plague' of prostitution was, as it has been throughout history, spread across all areas and societies, with even the smallest of towns having their own particular red-light areas. Let us take a look at somewhere a little more 'average' than a bustling port city; a small yet rapidly developing town that grew up on the banks of the Severn at a geographically advantageous location near the Welsh border.

Present day Shrewsbury is a relatively affluent town in Shropshire, sitting close to the border with Wales. With museums and university campuses aplenty to suit its aspirational middle England air, the town centre is almost entirely circled by the River Severn, which keeps its prize catch bound in a tight liquid loop. In the mid-1800s the riverside area that is still known as Roushill was home to some of the more colourful of the town's inhabitants. Bordered by Roushill Bank and Mardol and set, as it still is, alongside the river and next to the Welsh Bridge – the main route for those following Watling Street (now the A5 trunk road) to Wales and Ireland – nineteenth-century Roushill was the perfect setting for the 'ladies of the night'.

River trade had long been handled on the banks of the Severn alongside Roushill's lower border, with Roushill Bank and Mardol containing the closest public houses for barge workers looking for a break. The Globe is long gone but the Kings Head is still open as a public house, its crooked frontage little changed since it was first built back in the fifteenth century. The area had many 'shuts' – passages – linking streets and buildings, making it a hive of busy and overcrowded living. Poor sewerage combined with the adjacent river regularly flooding into surrounding streets meant that the town had long developed a topographically literal 'upper versus lower' system of living.

The higher ground in Shrewsbury is historically the more affluent, as it is in many towns and cities. The basic laws of physics meant that in the time before modern drainage systems it was always better to live uphill of potential effluent. Higher ground therefore became both more covetable *and* expensive. The lower areas were lower in all senses: places such as Frankwell (just over the Welsh Bridge and historically out of the town's control) and Roushill itself were more likely to be swamped by the river (and sewage), making them the cheapest and most accessible areas for the poorest of the town's inhabitants.

The population of Shrewsbury increased rapidly as the century wore on, particularly after the railway station opened in 1848, connecting the town to Chester and then to Wolverhampton. Inevitably there was never going to be enough legitimate employment available for all those who ended up living in the county town. When you consider that the age of consent at the time was still only twelve years old, it's not difficult to see how vulnerable girls and young women may have had no option but to take the simplest solution when it came to getting money in their pockets. Small town or big city, the story is generally the same.

Believed to be the last town in Britain to still have a street called Grope Lane – which started out as Gropecunt Lane, a name that really was meant literally – the town's mediaeval architecture, tiny shuts and alleyways made it easy for illicit encounters to go unnoticed in the darkness.

The reason that Shrewsbury makes such an interesting case study is that, in the 1861 census return for the Roushill area of the town, enumerator Thomas Darlington chose to list prostitutes and brothel-keepers as precisely what they were, rather than using the then-common euphemisms of 'seamstress' or 'milliner'. Thus, we read of Sarah Jones keeping a brothel in Masons Passage and Margaret Morris of Kings Head Shut, who gives her occupation as 'lodging house keeper' but nevertheless has 'brothel' written and underlined beneath her address by the returning officer (who clearly knew the area well). Mary Anthony, a thirty-year-old in the same trade, had four young ladies living under her Roushill roof, ranging in age from eighteen to twenty seven. On the date of the census, Anthony's 'girls' also had two young gentlemen staying with them – one aged nineteen, the other twenty two – who were clearly loathe to give any identifying details, appearing on the records only as 'Visitors, condition n/k'.

In addition to those who were listed openly, it's probable that many of the women listed on the census as 'dressmakers' were almost certainly also prostitutes and simply more practiced in the art of subtlety. However sleepy nineteenth-century Shrewsbury may have seemed in comparison to the bigger cities that were moving into reach with the improved transport system, the problems associated with prostitution and promiscuity were no different. In June 1854 the *Shrewsbury Chronicle* reported that renowned local prostitute Mary Watkins – a 'notorious character' – had been sentenced to twelve months hard labour for stealing from a Thomas Davies. Considering that Mary had no defence counsel and that the sentence was to be her twelfth jail term, one has to consider how much of a struggle her life must have been in the 'real' world for her to keep risking imprisonment.

As in many other towns and cities with a prostitution 'problem', Shrewsbury had its own dedicated rehab centre. Salop Penitentiary sat in St Julian's Friars, behind what is now an audio retail centre. Founded in 1865, the home had been funded by public subscription in order to replace its original premises a few short yards away on Dogpole (listed on the 1861 census as a 'Penitentiary for outcast females'), which had been rapidly outgrown. Precious little information survives about what was eventually renamed The Salop Home, as Victorian town councils were not very forthcoming when it came to recording those less salubrious aspects of the town's habits. From what we do know, it appears that the Shrewsbury home was perhaps less successful than its city cousin in Highgate. Though it was claimed that 'two thirds' of its inmates went on to lead productive, 'respectable' lives, anecdotal evidence suggests that life in the penitentiary was extremely harsh and it wasn't unusual for women to escape before their prescribed stay was up, presumably returning to their old ways in Shrewsbury's narrow shuts.

Whether town or city, there were few places untouched by the sex trade in Victorian Britain; much like today.

Chapter 8

A Walk on the Wilde Side

Homosexuality in Victorian Britain

In April 1870 Hugh Alexander Mundell visited the Surrey Theatre on Blackfriars Road, London. Later to describe himself as leading an 'idle' life, Mundell liked to style himself a gentleman, but was in reality merely the son of a barrister who lived with his widowed father in Pimlico, an area which, at the time, was in something of a decline. Naive as Mundell undoubtedly was, it is unlikely that he didn't realise there was something out of the ordinary about the two young men who entered the theatre bar. Informed by the manager that they were, in fact, women dressed as men, Mundell was seemingly mesmerised, to the extent of following them out of the theatre and into to a nearby tavern. But the theatre manager had been wrong. In reality, the pair were, biologically at least, as male as Mundell himself.

Thomas Ernest Boulton and Frederick William Park had been moderately successful as a double act, performing as 'Stella Clinton and Fanny Winifred Park'. So good, in fact, were their female disguises that on one occasion they were arrested, and eventually bound over to keep the peace, after being mistaken for women dressed as men.

One can, therefore, understand Mundell's confusion at being confronted by such a deliciously different double act. Whatever his true beliefs or motivation, the fact is that Mundell appreciated Boulton and Park enough to accompany them to the theatre on the evening of 28 April 1870, with the duo dressed in full female regalia. Unfortunately for our happy little band of friends, they were spotted on their travels by a police detective. Following them to the Strand Theatre, the nosy sleuth observed them meeting two other men before the entire party disappeared into a private box.

As the group left the theatre, the police pounced. Two of them managed to escape, but Boulton, Park and Mundell were arrested and taken to Bow Street police station, where they sat shivering together overnight in a cell, uncertain as to their fate.

As it turned out, their immediate fate was uncertain, though assuredly unpleasant. Mundell – who had stuck to his story that he believed Boulton and Park to be women, regardless of what clothes they wore – was granted bail. Fanny and Stella – already being called the 'He-She Ladies' by the fascinated media – were treated rather less favourably. Refused a change of clothes (an associate had in fact brought men's clothing to the police station for the pair to change into, but had been turned away), they had no choice but to appear in the dock in the dresses they had worn to the theatre the previous evening and also slept in while in the cells. Remanded in custody for a period of seven days, they were immediately taken off to a dingy room where a police surgeon was waiting to examine them.

Dr James Paul's task was a straightforward one; to ascertain whether the prisoners had been involved in the crime of buggery, which at the time carried a penalty of life imprisonment. Harsh as this sounds, Fanny and Stella were lucky; buggery had carried the death penalty until a mere nine years previously. One can only imagine how scared and intimidated the pair felt as they were made, one at a time, to remove their clothes, bend over and submit their most intimate of areas for close inspection.

Dr Paul's report declared him 'shocked' by what he found, and he described in detail 'very much dilated' and 'rough' anuses. He had no doubt whatsoever that the prisoners had been involved in the act of buggery and that they should be charged accordingly.

Amazingly, it appears to have not occurred to either Boulton or Park to flee while awaiting trial. Some have suggested that the pair might have been so naive that they didn't truly comprehend the potential consequences of any convictions. They eventually appeared in front of the Lord Chief Justice, Sir Alexander Cockburn, in early May 1871. Cockburn was, perhaps surprisingly for the time, highly critical of the prosecution and particularly of the behaviour of the police involved in the case. The intrusive physical examinations inflicted during the initial arrests also brought some considerable level of support from the general public. The prosecution failed to assemble a strong enough case and, despite the medical investigation, there was no legal proof that either Fanny or Stella had taken part in any acts of buggery. Furthermore, it was established in the trial that there was no offence in English law that specifically forbade the wearing of women's clothes by men. Fanny and Stella were duly found not guilty.

Fanny left Britain for New York, before dying at the tender age of thirty-four in 1881, almost certainly of complications from syphilis. Stella changed her name to Ernest Byne and continued to tour as a female impersonator, alongside her brother, Gerard. Ernest died in 1904 in Holborn, London, at the age of fifty-six.

In September 1880 the Association of Pawnbrokers' Assistants hired the Temperance Hall in York Street, Hulme, for the purposes of holding a fancy dress ball. This wouldn't have been anything out of the ordinary; had the APA known anything about it. When police raided the event, after a tip-off that all might not be quite as it seemed, they were confronted with panicked chaos. The guests scattered, and men dressed in their best party frocks attempted to escape through the windows, only to be pulled back into the room by the many officers who had been sent to intervene. The musical act at the event – a blind harmonium player from Manchester by the name of Mark Letcha – stood motionless in the corner, presumably wondering what act of madness was suddenly going on around him.

Police reports after the event noted that it was *very* convenient that Mr Letcha was unable to see what kind of company he was keeping, as he clearly could not be expected to testify in court. One might suspect that his sightlessness was perhaps the main attraction when the group chose which entertainment to book for the evening.

Later described as 'one of the foulest and most disgraceful orgies that ever disgraced any town', the guests apparently 'danced some strange kind of dance, in which they kicked their legs about a great deal ... In addition to the persons dancing, there were others sitting on benches round the room who engaged in the same indecent practices.' It is rather difficult to imagine what manner of immoral horrors could be prompted by the act of kicking one's legs around, but clearly the Manchester police took a very dim view of it.

Forty-seven men were arrested and their full names, ages, addresses and occupations printed in the newspapers for all to see. Bail was refused – even for those whose solicitors appealed for mercy on the grounds that they were 'men of good position' – the presiding magistrate declaring that 'he did not feel inclined to grant the prisoners any favour whatsoever, and he had no sympathy at all for them.'

The *Manchester Evening News* was, apparently, utterly bemused by the whole affair, reporting that many people attended the court hearings out of sheer curiosity as to why anyone would even be interested in such a strange pastime. 'The idea of a ball [...] without ladies seemed so incongruous and so incomplete that some curiosity was felt to see men who could manage to extract enjoyment out of so tame an entertainment.' The same reporter also noted that 'several of them made very good-looking women.'

All of the men were eventually released on payment of sureties, the court apparently deciding that it wasn't in the public interest to publicise such activities any further. However, it is doubtful that any of the accused was ever allowed to forget.

In the summer of 1889, fifteen-year-old Charles Swinscow was stopped for questioning by a constable from the General Post Office's internal police force, who was investigating theft from the London Central Telegraph Office. Swinscow worked as a messenger boy for the LCTO and, on being searched, was found to have money in his pocket equivalent to several weeks' wages. The messenger boys were forbidden from carrying cash of any amount while on duty in order to avoid it being muddled up with that belonging to customers, so Swinscow was immediately suspected of being responsible for the theft.

But Swinscow had earned his money. His explanation as to exactly *how* he'd earned it was to cause ripples of panic to spread among Britain's elite, all terrified that their secret lives were about to be uncovered. Swinscow confessed to police that he had been paid four shillings a time to 'go to bed with gentlemen' at an address in Fitzrovia. And he wasn't alone. It rapidly became clear that several of the GPO's other messenger boys were supplementing their income in the same way.

The house at 19 Cleveland Street no longer officially exists, but in the late 1800s the address in Fitzrovia was the home of one Charles Hammond, alleged brothel-keeper. Hammond had a tip-off that his property was under surveillance after Swinscow's questioning and he fled to France, never to return.

The biggest potential scandal connected to the Cleveland Street affair was the list of Hammond's alleged clients, who were said to include none other than Prince Albert Victor, Duke of Clarence and Avondale and a grandson of Queen Victoria. Several of the messenger boys had also named Lord Arthur Somerset, equerry to the prince's father, as a regular client of the brothel. Somerset was brought in for questioning in early August 1889. Although there are no surviving records of the interview, it is known that a report was issued advising that a prosecution should be brought against him for crimes under Section 11 of the Criminal Law Amendment Act 1885.

It is alleged that Somerset gave police the initials P. A. V., who, he said, was a fellow client of 19 Cleveland Street. Whether or not the letters stood for Prince Albert Victor has never been officially proven, but Somerset was told that the case against him would be dropped, at least temporarily. He subsequently made a generous – but risky – move in arranging for his own solicitor to act on behalf of the boys who had been implicated in the case. When the police began to take a new interest in him after his intervention, Somerset decided that discretion was, after all, the better part of valour and fled to Europe.

It is often reported that the telegraph boys themselves were given light sentences, and this is used as 'proof' that homosexuality was seen at the time as an upper-class vice inflicted on those naive lower-class men and boys who were unfortunate enough to get dragged in. But the term 'light' is relative. Although the boys were sentenced to serve between four and nine months behind bars – less than half the term generally imposed for gross indecency at the time – it was still 'hard labour'. Despite their age and circumstance, the telegraph boys certainly didn't get off lightly.

For a large part of British history, no one was particularly interested in what went on behind bedroom doors, or even who it went on with, and there are relatively few records of people being punished for their sexual behaviour. This may simply be, however, a combination of poor record-keeping and the fact that such matters were dealt with by the church rather than the state.

It wasn't until the sixteenth century that any major legal restrictions were enforced, and when they were, they were draconian. Pushed through Parliament by Thomas Cromwell, the Buggery Act of 1533 was aimed at 'the detestable and abominable Vice of Buggery committed with Mankind or Beast' (although what the term 'buggery' itself actually specified wasn't defined any further than that). This was the era of King Henry VIII and his determination to take power – and property – back from the Church.

Up until this point priests and monks had been relatively safe from fabricated criminal charges as they could not be hanged, even if they committed murder. They were not, however, safe from the Buggery Act. Anyone convicted under the new act could be hanged, with their land and property subject to confiscation by the government. The act was, therefore, almost inevitably used with depressing regularity against suspects who were almost certainly not guilty of an offence; they just happened to own property that the king fancied for himself.

Sodomy (although the etymology is slightly different, buggery and sodomy are generally used interchangeably when referring to anal sex) had been punishable by the death penalty until 1861, when the Offences Against the Person Act replaced it with ten years' imprisonment. The last hangings for the crime had occurred some time earlier, in November 1835, when John Smith and James Pratt were put to death at Newgate Prison. Police had been called to the rented rooms of a third man, William Bonill, by his suspicious landlord, who alleged to have peered through the keyhole in Bonill's door and witnessed 'sexual intimacy' between Smith and Pratt. Bonill, as party to such an act, was transported to Van Diemen's Land (now Tasmania) in 1835 and died there five years later.

The poet and playwright Michael Field had his big break in 1884, when *The Spectator* published a triumphantly flattering review of his play 'Fair Rosamund', declaring him to be 'a new voice, which is likely to be heard far and wide among the English-speaking people'. Other critics agreed, some even going so far as to declare Field 'the new Shakespeare'. The only question mark hanging over Field's work was that no one quite knew who he was. This new voice had seemingly sprung from nowhere and appeared on the literary scene somehow fully formed. This piqued the curiosity of renowned writer Robert Browning, who wrote to Field enquiring as to whether he might be kind enough to give Browning some details of his background. Field eventually agreed, explaining that not only was Michael Field not a real person, he wasn't even a 'he', and there were two of them.

Katharine Bradley and Edith Cooper were an unlikely writing partnership. Born in 1862, Cooper was the daughter of Katharine's older sister, Emma, whose health began to fail after the birth of her second child, leading Katharine to become her niece's legal guardian. Regardless of family connections, by the time Edith was studying at Bristol University in the 1870s, the pair were living together as both a romantic couple and writing partners.

The women let Browning in on their secret on the proviso that he was absolutely discreet about their true identities. Unfortunately for them, their confidante was loose-lipped and the truth came out; 'Michael Field' was no more. Critical opinion turned on its sexist axis; not only were the 'great works' written by women, the very idea of writing partnerships (of whatever combination of gender) were looked down upon, the implication being that neither author was talented enough to work alone.

Financially independent, courtesy of an inheritance after the death of Edith's father, the pair lived out their lives quietly with their beloved dog, Whym Chow, for whom they wrote a book of poems. They died within a year of each other and are buried together in Mortlake, Richmond upon Thames.

It will be noted that legal judgment was passed only on activities occurring between men. Women are completely ignored in homosexuality legislation (the term 'gay' to describe same-sex partnerships didn't come into general use until the mid-twentieth century) and legal issues around sapphic love rarely grace the pages of history books.

It's often said that this is because Queen Victoria simply couldn't bring herself to imagine that women might do such a thing and therefore refused to accept that lesbianism even existed, let alone as a problem significant enough to warrant a law against it. Sadly for the myth-makers, this theory – along with the oft-repeated quote 'Women do not do such things' – is not only fabricated, it is also surprisingly recent in its origin.

In March 1977 an activist group known as the 'Lesbians Ignite Fire Brigade' held a protest in honour of International Women's Day, at the site of a statue of Queen Victoria, in Wellington, New Zealand. The statue was draped with a banner reading 'Lesbians Are Everywhere' and when asked their motives, the group replied that Victoria had 'denied the existence' of lesbians. This is the first record of the theory ever being mentioned publicly and is far more likely to have been a spur-of-the-moment explanation from someone put on the spot by a news team. There are many records of Victoria's thoughts and opinions, both from her own diaries and parliamentary records. Had she voiced an opinion on the legalities of lesbianism there would inevitably be hard evidence, but none has been found. Even if the then-queen felt strongly about such things, it is very unlikely that she would have meddled with Parliament's work. Acts of Parliament have always required 'Royal Assent' in order to pass into law, but in practice this is merely a formality. It is almost unheard of for a monarch to disagree with or refuse to sign an assent.

It is far more likely that MPs simply decided against including lesbianism in legislation for fear of drawing attention to it and giving women 'ideas'. This belief, that it wouldn't occur to the fairer sex to dally with female company unless men suggested it, was reinforced during the reign of Victoria's grandson, George V, in 1921, when an amendment intended to make 'gross acts of indecency' illegal between women was rejected by the House of Lords. In his argument that allowing it through would only draw attention to the possibilities, the Earl of Malmesbury said, 'The more you advertise vice by prohibiting it the more you will increase it.' (Hansard, 15 August 1921 (accessed 29 December 2018)).

Men were not to be let off so lightly. The year 1885 saw the passing of the Criminal Law Amendment Act. On the surface a broadly positive political move made in order to protect women, it was one with an unexpected – and very last minute – inclusion; an inclusion that would later prove to be the downfall of Oscar Wilde.

The Criminal Law Amendment Act itself was almost entirely concerned with offences against women and girls. It even carried the subtitle, 'An Act to make further provision for the Protection of Women and Girls, the suppression of brothels, and other purposes.' The fact that it was entirely female-centric makes it all the more surprising that it is remembered more for its impact on men.

Henry Labouchère was perhaps an unlikely moral warrior. The son of a banker, Labouchère junior inherited a sizeable fortune after the death of his uncle, Whig politician Henry Labouchère, 1st Baron Taunton.

Notorious for his gambling habits while at Cambridge, Labouchère's degree was withheld after accusations of cheating. He joined the diplomatic service, but was perhaps not best suited to diplomacy as an art: he famously responded to the Foreign Secretary's offer of the position of Second Secretary of Her Majesty's Legation in Buenos Aires, with the rather pompous response, 'I beg to state that, if residing at Baden-Baden I can fulfil those duties, I shall be pleased to accept the appointment.' The German town of Baden-Baden being somewhat distant from Argentina, the offer was rescinded and Labouchère informed that his services were no longer required.

After a brief stint as a Liberal MP, Labouchère's thoughts turned to the stage. Along with business partners, he engaged renowned architect C.J. Phipps to create the Queen's Theatre in Long Acre, Covent Garden (the theatre survived for little more than a decade and was demolished; a residential block now stands on the site). His theatrical exploits brought Labouchère into contact with the actress Henrietta Hodson. The couple began a long affair and lived together out of wedlock for twenty-one years until Hodson's husband died in 1887, finally leaving them free to marry.

Given his generally libertarian views and outré lifestyle, it may come as a surprise that Labouchère was not only a virulent anti-semite who opposed all forms of feminism, he was also a determined homophobe. In 1887 he founded the weekly journal *Truth* as a platform for his views and – luckily for him, if no one else – had the funds available to fight the endless court cases that arose from his declarations. Unpleasant spats included those with such notorious characters as Edward Levy-Lawson, owner of *The Daily Telegraph*, and that well-known writer of comic operas, W.S. Gilbert, who had incurred Labouchère's wrath by publicly feuding with Hodson.

Labouchère returned to politics in 1880 as the Liberal MP for Northampton. In 1885 the Criminal Law Amendment Act was finally going through Parliament, political stalling having dragged it out for several years, primarily due to the public outcry caused by W.T. Stead's campaign against child prostitution in *The Pall Mall Gazette*. Stead had written to Labouchère from jail, after he was imprisoned for his part in the Maiden Tribute case, warning of a perceived increase in male prostitution across London and other major British cities. Homophobic feelings were running high, stoked in part by such journals as the

Yokel's Preceptor (sub-titled *The Greenhorn's Guide thro' Little Lunnon*), which, in 1855, published the following advice to its readers:

A FEW WORDS ABOUT MARGERIES
The Way To Know The Beasts – Their Haunts, &C.

The increase of these monsters in the shape of men, commonly designated *Margeries, Pooffs, &c.*, of late years, in the great metropolis, renders it necessary for the safety of the public, that they should be made known … Will the reader credit it, but such is nevertheless the fact, that these monsters actually walk the streets the same as the whores, looking out for a chance! … Yes, the Quadrant, Fleet-street, Holborn, the Strand, &c., are actually thronged with them! Nay, it is not long since, in the neighbourhood of Charing Cross, they posted bills in the windows of several respectable public houses, cautioning the public to "Beware of Sods!" … We could relate many instance of the gross bestiality of the practices of these wretches, but think it would be occupying too much of the reader's time on so disgusting a subject.

Of course, the *Preceptor* then goes on to tell its poor reader in quite some detail about said 'disgusting subject'. The problem was that the *Preceptor* wasn't the moralistic journal it purported to be. Published by one 'H. Smith' of Holywell Street, the address in itself should have been a clue. Holywell Street was, as we know, London's pornographic centre at the time. 'H. Smith' was, in reality, the infamous William Dugdale, whose pornographic publishing habits we have already discussed.

Sold in effect as a guide to the capital's best pick-up joints – the section on the habits of homosexual men is actually very small in comparison to the detailed information about the best gambling houses and which female prostitutes one should keep a look out for – the *Preceptor* was firmly tongue in cheek and intended as titillation rather than dire warning.

But Stead and Labouchère saw it as further proof that the country's morals were being flushed down the drain faster than waste through the brand new sewerage system underneath the capital. With his ire stoked by Stead and a determination to clean up this perceived curse of filthy behaviour, Labouchère decided to add an amendment to this legislation for the protection of females, in order to bring male behaviour into line. Late in the evening of Thursday, 6 August 1885, Labouchère proposed an extra clause to the act that was going through the House: 'Any male person who, in public or private, commits, or is a party to the commission of, or procures, or attempts to procure the commission by any male person of, any act of gross indecency with another male person, shall be guilty of a misdemeanour, and being convicted thereof, shall be liable at the discretion of the Court to be imprisoned for any term not exceeding two years, with or without hard labour.'

The addition, which would eventually become Section 11 of the final act, is notable for two things: the lack of definition as to what specifically constitutes 'gross indecency', and also the caveat 'in public or private'. In effect, a man could now be accused of gross indecency for simply being found in the company of another male in his own home. All it took was a third person to decide they seemed a bit too familiar with each other and report it to the authorities.

'Gross indecency' was generally interpreted to mean any intimate act between two men which stopped short of actual sodomy. Prosecutions for gross indecency were therefore likely to have a much higher success rate than those for sodomy, as they required less proof and carried a relatively lesser punishment. The vagueness of the term meant that men were at very real risk of vindictive false accusations.

One of the most renowned cases to be brought under the auspices of Labouchère's amendment to the Criminal Law Amendment Act was that of Regina vs. Wilde, held at the Old Bailey in the spring of 1895. Encouraged by his young lover, Alfred 'Bosie' Douglas, Oscar Wilde had attempted to sue Douglas's father, the Marquess of Queensberry, in March of that year, after the marquess had left a calling card at Wilde's club, the Abermarle, reading 'For Oscar Wilde, posing somdomite' (sic).

Queensberry certainly had an axe to grind, but it wasn't necessarily with Wilde; he was just an easier target onto which the marquess could vent his paternal grief and anger. Queensberry's eldest son, and Bosie's brother, Francis, Viscount Drumlanrig, had died at the age of just twenty-seven in October 1894, after what was reported as a 'hunting accident'. Suspected of having had a homosexual relationship with the then-prime minister, Archibald Primrose, Earl of Rosebery, Francis' death was widely believed, in reality, to have been suicide, or even possibly murder. Queensberry wasn't prepared to watch another of his beloved sons head down the same dangerous path and perhaps saw in Wilde an opportunity for vengeance against the tragedy that had befallen Francis.

When Wilde decided to sue for libel, the marquess saw his chance. Wilde's action against Queensberry was ill-advised by anyone's standards. If the marquess could prove that he was telling the truth and that Wilde was indeed a 'sodomite', not only would the case be thrown out, it would also leave the way open for Wilde himself to be prosecuted under Section 11 of the Criminal Law Amendment Act. But proceed Wilde did, only to be forced into dropping the case swiftly when Queensberry's defence counsel announced that he had found 'several' male prostitutes who would testify that they had had sex with Wilde.

Almost immediately after Wilde left the court, a warrant was issued for his arrest for the crime of gross indecency. He was advised by friends to flee to France, but the fight had gone out of him. Declaring, 'the train has gone. It is too late', Wilde merely awaited his inevitable fate.

Arrested on 6 April 1895, Wilde was sent on remand to Holloway Prison to await trial. On 26 April, in front of Mr Justice Charles, Wilde pleaded not guilty to the charges against him. Eventually allowed bail – put up by the Reverend Stewart Headlam, an Anglican priest who disagreed with Wilde's treatment by both the courts and the press – Wilde fled to the home of his friends, Ada and Ernest Leverson. Ada was a renowned writer and close ally of Wilde (who nicknamed her 'Sphinx'), and risked both her professional and personal relationships in order to support her friend.

When the trial restarted under Mr Justice Wills at the end of May, it was clear from the outset that Wilde was to be made a thorough example of, as an illustration of the disgust in which Victorian society held homosexuality (at least, in public). Such was the treatment meted out to him that even Edward Carson, the head of Queensberry's defence counsel in the libel trial, approached Frank Lockwood, QC, the Solicitor General, and allegedly said, 'Can we not let up on the fellow now?' to which Lockwood replied that he would like to do so, but the case had become overly political and impossible to drop. Lockwood's position was possibly made firmer by the involvement in the case of his own nephew, Maurice Schwabe. Now thought to have been conducting his own affair with Alfred Douglas ahead of Wilde's prosecution, Schwabe had taken a conveniently timed trip to Sydney, Australia, and was never officially mentioned in the court case. A letter from Douglas to Schwabe dated 5 March 1893, in which Alfred address him as 'My darling Pretty' and describes himself as Schwabe's 'boy-wife', is held in the collection of the State Library, New South Wales.

Wilde was doomed from the start. Despite his infamous and impassioned speech about 'the love that dare not speak its name' – 'It is beautiful, it is fine, it is the noblest form of affection. There is nothing unnatural about it [...] The world mocks it and sometimes puts one in the pillory for it" – the prosecution was determined to let nothing stand between them and a conviction.

On 25 May 1895 Oscar Fingal O'Flahertie Wills Wilde was found guilty of gross indecency and sentenced to two years' hard labour. When told of the sentence, Henry Labouchère declared himself disappointed that it was so short and that he would have preferred his amendment to have carried a longer sentence.

Frail of health to start with, Wilde never recovered from his stint in gaol. After a period of decline, during which he spent what money he had on drink and hardly left his room, one of the greatest wits of modern times died in poverty in a cheap Parisian hotel room, on 30 November 1900.

Labouchère's late-night amendment would affect the lives of many over the following decades. By the time the Sexual Offences Act decriminalised homosexuality in 1967 (albeit for those over the age of twenty-one and in private only), countless men had seen their lives destroyed simply because they were attracted to others of the same gender.

'I have no doubt that we shall win [...] but the road is long, and red with monstrous martyrdoms. Nothing but the repeal of the Criminal Law Amendment Act would be any good.' Oscar Wilde, in a letter to George Ives, 21 March 1898.

Chapter 9

Hidden in Plain Sight

Sexual Subtexts in Art and Literature

The advancement of commercial printing processes during the nineteenth century brought books and newspapers to a genuinely mass audience for the first time. In addition, the increase in rail services across the country not only enabled print to be distributed to far flung places on a daily basis, it also had the side effect of leaving bored passengers needing something with which to occupy themselves while travelling through the country. Reading was the obvious answer to an increasingly literate population.

Newspapers delivered headlines, gossip and lurid descriptions of global events in much the same way as today's tabloids inform and entertain us. Paperback books brought romance and excitement into difficult and dull daily lives. Circulating libraries – through which members paid an annual subscription in return for borrowing books that they might otherwise have not be able to afford – also helped spread literature further and wider than it had ever been before. W.H. Smith began his commercial enterprise as a simple London news vendor, but saw the opportunities that rail travel offered, opening newsstands at many of the new railway stations and offering his own circulating library service that enabled the reader to borrow a book from one station and drop it at another at the end of their journey.

What was most sensational about the new wave of novelists that broke through during the 1900s was that many were women, in a time when female authors were still struggling to be taken seriously. Mary Shelley's *Frankenstein* had originally been published anonymously in 1818, when its author was only in her early twenties. Those who suspected the author might be female derided the book on that basis alone and it would be another five years before it was republished with Shelley's name displayed on the cover.

It's no great surprise then that the Brontë sisters – Charlotte, Emily and Anne – all chose to use male pseudonyms when starting out on their literary careers. In fact, when Charlotte initially struck success with *Jane Eyre* (writing as Currer Bell), she had to travel to London in order to prove in person to her own publisher who she really was. *Jane Eyre* was a commercial success, but received a mixed reception from critics – particularly as rumours spread that the author was, indeed, a woman. In Brontë's novel, Mr Rochester breaks accepted conventions of the time by interacting with Jane – his employee, and a woman to boot – as an equal. The fact that this outrage was suggested by a female author simply compounded the critics' bias. The eponymous heroine of the title was clearly too headstrong, sexual and downright real for contemporary literary circles. But she has proved an enduring heroine and one can only imagine what a breath of fresh air she was in an era of propriety and inequality.

Ellen Wood was one of the most successful authors of the era. Having taken up writing in her forties, her literary success helped support her family after the failure of her husband Henry's business interests. Wood's 1861 novel *East Lynne* is the best known of the more than thirty titles she published in her lifetime.

East Lynne was the epitome of what became known as 'sensation fiction': novels that drew on Gothic melodrama to tell tales of loose morals, murder and insanity and which were purposely designed to both shock and thrill their audience (W. S. Gilbert wrote the comic opera *A Sensation Novel* about the craze for such books). The story of the fall from grace of one Lady Isabel Carlyle, *East Lynne* is an unlikely tale of adultery, seduction and disguise. Having left her loving family to elope with the dashing Captain Levison, Lady Isabel bears his illegitimate child, only to realise rather belatedly that the captain has no intention of marrying her. But Lady Isabel is now a 'fallen woman', who has sinned and must therefore be punished for her failings both as a woman and as a mother.

And punished she most certainly is. Badly disfigured in a train crash that kills her illegitimate child, Isabel somehow manages to be taken on as governess to her own children without her husband – who has remarried, having secured a divorce in her absence – recognising the woman to whom he was married and who gave birth to their children in earlier, happier years. Not only does Isabel now have to watch from the sidelines as her husband plays happy families with her children and his new wife, she also nurses her own son as he dies from consumption, without once letting on who she really is. It is only on her deathbed that Isabel confesses to Carlyle who she is and that it was him she loved all along. But it's too late for Isabel, who made the mistake of being a woman with sexual urges, and for that she must pay. *East Lynne*'s scandalous storyline certainly paid off for Ellen Wood – or 'Mrs Henry Wood', as she preferred to be known – with an estimated half a million copies sold by the end of the century.

The Rossetti family vault in Highgate Cemetery, north London, might have romance in its history, but it is not particularly welcoming or elegant in the cold light of day. Only recently cleared enough to enable access, for years it was overgrown and excluded from even the most eager of visitor tours.

Those laid to rest in the family plot include poet Christina Rossetti, alongside Christina's parents, brother and sister-in-law. With them lie the mortal remains of Elizabeth 'Lizzie' Siddal, wife of Christina's oldest brother, the poet and artist Dante Gabriel Rossetti. The one person who isn't buried in the family grave is Dante himself.

The Pre-Raphaelite Brotherhood are now probably the best known of Victorian art and artists, yet they were not quite so popular in nineteenth-century artistic circles: their insistence on using realism rather than flattery in their work made some viewers uncomfortable. Charles Darwin declared the John Everett Millais painting *Christ in the House of His Parents* to be both ugly and blasphemous, showing the holy family as a little too real (for which, read 'poor') for contemporary tastes.

The Pre-Raphaelites were a loose and shifting collective of artists, sculptors and poets. Some were successful in more than one field; Dante Gabriel Rossetti was a noted poet as well as an artist whose influence carried on through many later generations. The art of the Pre-Raphaelites was heavily influenced by mediaevalism and carried an air of barely disguised sensuality, as well as a sharp eye for socio-political commentary. William Holman Hunt's *The Awakening Conscience* (1853) is, on the surface, an adept illustration of a couple perhaps in the middle of an argument, or playing flirtatious games. But a closer look at the detail and symbolism within the painting tell a very different story.

The woman wears no wedding band, yet is clearly on intimate terms with the man who is pulling her down onto his lap. The assumption, then, is that she is his mistress. We can see in the mirror on the wall behind the couple that she is looking out through a window onto sunlight and freedom, but the room itself is gaudy; over-decorated and claustrophobic. A shaft of light picks out tangled threads that have fallen to the floor and a dropped glove signals the hurriedness of their assignation. Some interpret the woman's movement as recognition of the error of her ways and a situation from which she must free herself; a theory borne out by the predatory cat that has been tucked into a corner of the painting, playing with a delicate bird that is frantically trying to escape.

Art and literature have long had the freedom to discuss subjects that polite society deemed too troublesome, veiling uneasy thoughts with words and oil paints. This is exceedingly useful to those of us looking back through time at a previous era, because it enables us – if we look very carefully – to see what was really going on beneath the thin and fragile veneer of propriety. Thus, artists such as Holman Hunt were able to illustrate the social issues around mistresses and the inequality of the sexes.

John Collier's *Lilith* (cover image) portrays the first wife of Adam – created by God from the same clay out of which Adam was formed – consorting with over-large, swollen serpents. Expelled from the Garden of Eden for refusing to submit to Adam's will, on the sound principle that they were made the same and therefore should be considered equal, Collier's Lilith is powerful and unashamed of her nakedness, showing no fear of the giant snakes wrapping themselves sinuously around her body. In this one painting, Collier comments on religion, equality and sexuality in a way that would never have been possible verbally.

Sexuality was a large part of the Pre-Raphaelite agenda. Nothing illustrates this more clearly than the story of the famed PRB model and muse Elizabeth 'Lizzie' Siddal. A milliner's assistant by trade, Elizabeth began modelling for William Deverall in 1849 and through him became acquainted with the rest of the Pre-Raphaelites. Her dedication to the artistic cause was almost Lizzie's downfall. While modelling for Sir John Everett Millais' renowned *Ophelia* in 1852, she lay in a bath of water that was heated by oil lamps while Millais worked on his painting. Lost in concentration, Millais failed to notice that the lamps had gone out and Siddal didn't tell him. She developed pneumonia and it is said that Millais felt responsible enough to pay her ensuing medical bills. It's far more likely that he was intimidated into paying them by Siddal's furious father. It's even alleged in some quarters that Millais had the front to knock Mr Siddal down from the amount of compensation he originally requested.

Having met Dante Gabriel Rossetti while modelling for Deverall, Siddal became his model, his muse and his obsession. He put a stop to her modelling for other artists in order to focus on her himself and painted hundreds, possibly thousands of pictures of her. Always artistic herself, Siddal began to paint more earnestly after becoming engaged to Rossetti. Her career was subsidised by art critic John Ruskin, who paid Lizzie a retainer in order to take ownership of anything she created (and also to control her life to the point of supervising her healthcare and general wellbeing, as well as telling her when and when not to paint and in what style).

But this was the nineteenth century, with all its carefully delineated social divisions, and Rossetti's family was not impressed by his relationship with the lower-class Siddal. The son of scholarly parents and nephew of John William Polidori (author and associate of both Shelley and Byron), not to mention the brother of renowned poet Christina Rossetti, Dante Gabriel Rossetti was expected to do better for himself than to marry a working-class model. Siddal knew only too well the level of disregard in which she was held by her husband's family and it served to reinforce her (well-founded, it would transpire) fears that Rossetti would eventually tire of her and replace her with a newer model. Never strong in health, Lizzie grappled with depression and an addiction to laudanum, her struggles exacerbated by both her husband's unfaithfulness and the stillbirth of their baby daughter in 1861. Suffering from postnatal depression and already pregnant again so soon after her previous loss, Elizabeth Siddal died from an overdose of laudanum on 11 February 1862, at the age of only thirty-two.

It is widely accepted that Siddal intended to die; Rossetti allegedly found a suicide note pinned to her clothes. But as well as being considered a crime, suicide also barred the deceased from a Christian burial and brought shame onto any surrounding family. It is believed that the guilty and grief-stricken Rossetti took the letter to his close friend Ford Maddox Brown, who advised him to throw it onto the fire. The coroner's inquest duly ruled Siddal's death to have been accidental.

Rossetti had his tragic wife interred in the family plot in Highgate Cemetery, where to this day she lies amongst the remains of the family who so openly disliked her. Believing that the death of his muse meant the death of his poetry, Rossetti tucked some of his own poems – the only copy of a collection he had been labouring over for several years – under Lizzie's long, auburn hair before her coffin was closed.

Seven years later, and struggling with a severe bout of writer's block, he began to regret his grand gesture. Encouraged by his business-minded agent, Charles Augustus Howell, Rossetti decided to have Lizzie's body disinterred in order to recover the lost works. Rather poetically, when the gruesome task was complete and Rossetti received his papers back after being disinfected, they had been damaged by both water and insects and were mostly illegible.

Struggling with guilt and grief, Rossetti was, for many years, obsessed with the idea that Lizzie was haunting him. He regularly had a clairvoyant visit him at home and chose to believe that the table rapping noises through the medium's sessions was his lost muse speaking to him. Her myth had been perpetuated by Howell (who had been present at the disinterment, Rossetti himself not having had the stomach for it) attempting to comfort his client by insisting that not only had Lizzie's body not decayed in the slightest during the years she had been underground, her red hair had also continued to grow, filling her coffin with copper curls.

Rossetti clearly fretted that his dead wife and unborn child were waiting for him, and he couldn't be sure that their welcome would be a friendly one. He had a clause written into his will that he was under no circumstances to be buried in the family vault; which is how Lizzie Siddal came to lie with those who didn't want her, while her husband rests a safe seventy-five miles away in the seaside village of Birchington-on-Sea, in Kent.

For all the intense sensuality of the Pre-Raphaelite Brotherhood's artistic endeavours, the pretence of adoration of women is often just that; pretence. To the outwardly glamorous and sensual artists, women were still objects; beautiful, fragile objects that were treated with veneration, but objects nonetheless. And when the objects had served their purpose, they were disposed of and/or replaced.

'Victorian Gothic' is a well-known literature genre that has its roots in the eighteenth century with the publication of Horace Walpole's *The Castle of Otranto* (1764). It was named for the mediaeval Gothic architecture that is the setting for many of the genre's novels. The stories are dark and dangerous with a paranormal air.

What could be more visceral, violent and downright sexual than a vampire on a mission? Although the first modern vampire story to be published is widely accepted to have been *The Vampyre* by Dante Rossetti's uncle, John Polidori, its most famous example is that most Victorian of Gothic anti-heroes, Bram Stoker's *Dracula*.

Published in 1897, there is a strong sexual theme throughout Stoker's story, from the literal penetration of fangs into tender necks to the exchange of bloody bodily fluids that is needed for Dracula to convert his victims into fellow bloodsuckers. The most obvious moral parable within *Dracula* is the contrast drawn between the quiet and virtuous Mina Harker and her feisty, lustful friend, Lucy Westenra. The Lilith to Mina's Eve, Lucy refuses to bow to convention, discusses her suitors in what is portrayed as an indecent manner and is delightfully unrepentant in the face of disapproval. As the vampire's influence creeps over her, Lucy becomes increasingly animalistic and hungry, both physically and sexually.

Of course, poor disposable Lucy is merely a stepping-stone on Dracula's path towards reclaiming Mina, who he believes to be the reincarnation of his long-lost beloved. While Lucy transforms into a child-killing vampire who gets staked by the very men who profess to love her, Mina – described as having a man's brain and a woman's heart, because presumably that was the best combination to the Victorian mind – is forced into tasting the vampire's blood and consistently portrayed as a corrupted innocent. Whereas Lucy was bold and overtly sexual, thus presumably somehow deserving of her morbid fate, Mina is fighting the darkness like a good girl, even as she sinks deeper and more willingly into vampirism.

In *Dracula,* Stoker touches on many topics that were otherwise taboo in polite Victorian society. There is the temptation of pre-marital sex, with unmarried Lucy clearly not averse to at least having a taste of the fruit before she commits to eating it for the rest of her life. We have adultery, as Jonathan is – not entirely unwillingly – seduced by the trio of female vampires while trapped in the count's castle. Polyandry also makes an appearance, when Van Helsing suggests that Lucy might be considered a wife to each of the four men who gave her their blood in the vain attempt to save her life. In fact, in a letter to Mina, written before she is infected by the count, Lucy bewails, 'Why can't they let a girl marry three men, or as many as want her?'

Van Helsing goes so far as to declares himself a bigamist, as by giving Lucy his blood he has, in effect, been unfaithful to his deceased wife, to whom – in the eyes of the Church – he is still married.

Stoker makes no attempt to censor *Dracula*'s sexual elements in order to fit in with expected Victorian mores. Every character in the story is affected in some physically and/or mentally intrusive way by the count's malign influence. The vampire overpowers people – both male and female – and forces desire upon them until they cannot help but crave not only blood, but also the count himself. In effect, Dracula simply pulls each character's innate personality to the surface.

The story is also, at its core, one of sexual repression and vibrantly Victorian emotional rigidity. Jonathan Harker attempts to fight off the seduction of the three vampiric sister-whores while imprisoned in Dracula's castle, while at the same time desperately wanting to give in to it.

Mina herself is destined to become both Madonna *and* whore, torn between her lustful blood-link to Dracula and her ingrained desire to be a 'good girl'. When the men break into her room in order to save her, they indeed find her with the count. But instead of being the buttoned-up and prim young woman she has been portrayed in the book thus far, Mina is blood-smeared and dressed in white, having been drinking from the vampire while her husband lies unconscious on the floor next to them. Her vulnerability is almost shocking in its intimacy and the men race to cover and protect her (interestingly, in the 1992 film version by Francis Ford Coppola, Mina is absolutely intent in her determination to join her beloved count in the undead afterlife, a century of social change clearly having had an effect on how women's desire can be depicted).

And what of the count himself? Despite being cast in the role of villain, Dracula is essentially a tragic figure, doomed to spend all of eternity alone as an example of what happens when one doesn't follow a pure and righteous path (immortality not being a useful trait when it comes to making friends and establishing happy relationships). Grief and time may have hardened him into a misanthropic monster, but he is a monster towards whom the reader finds it hard to be entirely unsympathetic.

Reading *Dracula* with an eye to potential authorial motives, it is easy to assume that Stoker was comfortable with various forms of sexuality, both in person and on the page. The true story, however, was rather more complicated.

Bram Stoker and Oscar Wilde had known each other for many years prior to Dracula's publication. Stoker developed a friendship with the Wildes as a young adult and one of the most famous phrases in *Dracula* – 'children of the night' – was a description he'd originally seen used by Oscar's mother Jane in her 1887 book, *Ancient Legends, Mystic Charms, and Superstitions of Ireland.*

Wilde had courted noted beauty Florence Balcombe many years earlier, and was said to have been most upset when she eventually left him for Stoker, writing to Florence of the time they had spent together, 'the two sweet years – the sweetest years of all my youth'. However, the two men remained in touch even after the Stokers married and Dracula's creator was one of the few friends to visit Wilde in exile during the last years of his life.

Stoker's support of someone who had so publicly fallen from grace for the 'crime' of being attracted to his fellow men is interesting because he himself would later publicly denounce homosexuality. Historians have occasionally suggested that this was, in fact, a cover for Stoker's own sexual interest in men. Married or not, there is no question that Bram Stoker may well have been gay (a term which would have confused him at the time; 'gay' by this point in time generally translated as 'promiscuous', but it could be applied to either gender and was usually assumed to refer to heterosexual promiscuity, rather than same-sex activity).

Stoker is documented as having written a lengthy missive to poet Walt Whitman in 1872, in which he included a rather detailed list of his personal attributes: 'I am six feet two inches high and twelve stone weight naked and used to be forty-one or forty-two inches round the chest. I am ugly but strong and determined and have a large bump over my eyebrows. I have a heavy jaw and a big mouth and thick lips – sensitive nostrils – a snubnose and straight hair. I am equal in temper and cool in disposition and have a large amount of self control and am naturally secretive to the world.'

Of course, it's impossible to judge from a distance what Stoker's true motives for being so overtly personal with Whitman might have been, but there is a distinct air of homoeroticism in the detail of his personal description that cannot be denied. And Bram Stoker certainly wasn't averse to being something of an admirer of men throughout his life.

Stoker had a lengthy career as business manager of the Lyceum Theatre in London's West End, then under the ownership of Henry

Irving, an actor whose miserable marriage made him both bad tempered and prone to seeking out extracurricular romance (he was, allegedly, the long-term lover of famed actress Ellen Terry). The level of Irving and Stoker's closeness waxed and waned, dependent on the state of their working relationship, with Stoker clearly putting up with more bad behaviour from his employer than most would tolerate.

Stoker appeared to choose particular men to idolise at different periods of his life and, whether the relationships were ever physical or not, showed extreme loyalty to his chosen ones. In her article 'A Wilde Desire Took Me: The Homoerotic History of Dracula' (Johns Hopkins University Press, 1994), Talia Schaffer writes of Stoker's letter to Whitman: 'In its painfully intense frankness, especially its frankness about his inability to be frank, Stoker's love letter stands alone among all his writing. "I would like to call you Comrade and to talk to you as men who are not poets do not often talk. [...]" Stoker thanks Whitman, in the last line of his letter, for "all the love and sympathy you have given me in common with my kind." It is significant that Stoker believes he has a "kind" – that he belongs to a species set apart [...]'

Stoker's brand of devoted loyalty extended to Oscar Wilde, although there has never been any evidence to suggest that theirs was ever anything more than a platonic friendship. All this makes Stoker's later stand against homosexuality all the more surprising. Not long before his death in 1912, Bram Stoker called for all homosexual authors to be imprisoned.

Schaffer again: 'Stoker identifies with the national anti-Wilde homophobia, partly to disguise his own vulnerability as a gay man, partly because it justifies his belief in the value of the closet, and partly from horror at the monstrous image of Wilde produced by the media, which would haunt men of "his kind".'

One can only assume that the dying Stoker felt the need to assert his opposition to homosexuality before he went to the grave, lest he be denied the eternal rest that so long evaded his undead creation.

Dracula was, in fact, pre-dated by an even racier fictional vampire in *Carmilla*, Joseph Sheridan Le Fanu's 1872 tale of a bloodthirsty undead lesbian. Taking its themes from the religiously censorious social mores of the time, Le Fanu's creation was a huge influence on Stoker's more famous work. In the same way as Van Helsing would later appear in

Dracula, *Carmilla* uses Baron Vordenburg as a senior male role model who 'saves' the weak and waif-like women from the intimate and predatory danger that awaits them. The difference, of course, is that the danger is female in origin, and although Le Fanu never directly refers to sexuality in the text, it is heavily implied throughout. Although the later *Dracula* may appear on the surface to have taken its inspiration from *Carmilla*, it is more likely that both authors had heard similar folk tales and mythologies from previous centuries (vampires and other variants of the undead being a centuries-old trope in stories intended to frighten the reader).

There were also real-life stories to be adapted, including that of Elizabeth Bathory (1550-1614), a Hungarian countess who, to this day, is considered to be the most prolific female murderer of all time. Estimates suggest that Bathory may have tortured and killed several hundred young women, although the official body count was left at eighty, for lack of hard evidence.

The story of Bathory's horrific deeds were well known throughout the eighteenth and nineteenth centuries and it's very likely that both Le Fanu and Stoker knew the tales well.

In their hurry to romanticise the dark Victorian aesthetic, many subsequent historians have inadvertently coloured history themselves. We love to think of our old friend Oscar Wilde dying with a dramatic flounce in pleasingly beautiful poverty, swooning to his end after uttering the infamous phrase 'either that wallpaper goes or I do'. Luckily for those of us who love a dramatic wit, he did indeed say something similar: 'My wallpaper and I are fighting a duel to the death. One or other of us has to go.'

But Wilde's death was unlikely to have been anything approaching romantic. Now believed to have been killed by meningitis rather than the syphilis he long fretted that he carried but very probably didn't (there is no proof he was ever formally diagnosed with it), poor old Oscar died a horribly messy death, that almost certainly resulted from complications of a severe middle ear infection. While incarcerated in Wandsworth Prison, Wilde had collapsed and hit the hard floor, rupturing his right eardrum. Despite spending two months in the prison infirmary, the injury had never been properly treated and the pain from the developing infection haunted Wilde for the rest of his short life.

It says something of the grim physical realities of Wilde's demise that the sheets he'd lain on were burned and his body speedily buried, with the addition of a layer of quicklime to speed up decomposition. What his friends hadn't realised is that quicklime does not always have the destructive capabilities that horror stories would have us believe. When they decided to disinter Wilde's remains nine years later in order to re-inter him more thoughtfully, the body was well preserved. A witness was quoted as saying 'the teeth appeared lengthened.'

We now know that corpses often give the *appearance* of their hair and nails having continued to grow after death because of the shrinking back of the surrounding skin. But how temptingly lovely it would be to believe that a literally larger-than-life character such as Wilde might have joined Stoker's realm of the undead.

Even the most innocent of Victorian fiction often has darker undertones when we look back with knowing hindsight. Charles Lutwidge Dodgson (who, as an aside, was a friend of William Holman Hunt) is a case in point. When *Alice's Adventures in Wonderland* were published in 1865 under the pen name of Lewis Carroll, it was an enormous and rather unexpected success. But with fame came public curiosity and, over the intervening years, that curiosity has focused on Carroll's attachment to young girls; including the real-life Alice.

At the risk of disappointing any scandal-seekers, it is unlikely that either Charles Dodgson or, indeed, Lewis Carroll had any real sexual interest in Alice. This despite many fascinating and in-depth analyses of the book and its characters over the years, including this rather charming interpretation dating from 1933: 'Alice runs down the rabbit-hole after the White Rabbit and suddenly finds herself falling down "what seemed to be a very deep well." Here we have what is perhaps the best-known symbol of coitus.' (From *Alice in Wonderland Psychoanalysed* by A. M. E. Goldschmidt, quoted in *Aspects of Alice*, ed. Robert Phillips, p.281).

Goldschmidt was a writer rather than a qualified psychoanalyst, and given that he was writing in the 1930s, was perhaps simply following the contemporary fashion for Freudian interpretation. Nevertheless, this idea of Alice's creator as at least a potential 'dodgy uncle', if not a literal paedophile, stuck to Dodgson's reputation and has increasingly established itself as almost-fact over the intervening decades.

Those analysing Dodgson's motives were (and are) perhaps too quick to forget that genial bachelor 'uncles' were common during the Victorian era, often supervising friends' children (of all ages and sexes) with little or no question or supervision. This, of course, doesn't imply that all adult men/young child 'relationships' were innocent and/or acceptable, but what is certain is that nineteenth-century society definitely didn't apply the same levels of automatic suspicion that such attachments would attract today. The photography of nude children was also far less frowned upon than it is nowadays. 'Tasteful' prepubescent nudes appeared on postcards and in print as artistic portrayals of youthful innocence. Dodgson's photographic portrait of the real life Alice has a rather Lolita-ish air, but in reality is nothing more than a pretty image of a photogenic child.

But back to Carroll's adventures underground. Charles Dodgson was, in reality, something of a would-be lothario, his amorous inclinations almost entirely focusing on adult women. There is some contention as to whether Dodgson had a romantic interest in Alice's fourteen-year-old sister, Lorina, who, although a child to modern eyes, was above the legal age of consent (then only thirteen). In addition, some of Dodgson's own letters to potential paramours have survived. They show the author to be enthusiastic – if rather secretive – about his attraction to women.

Postscript

What Have The Victorians Ever Done For Us?

Queen Victoria's death on 22 January 1901 saw the end of the longest reign in British history (until 2015, when Elizabeth II surpassed her great-great-grandmother's record). It had been an era of huge social and economic changes and the country Victoria left behind her was completely different to the one she had taken control of more than sixty-three years earlier. The Queen was buried in a white dress and her wedding veil, and in her coffin were keepsakes from the men who had meant so much to her during her lifetime. She had left her physician, James Reid, with a list of carefully detailed instructions (which were preserved by his family after his own death), including the insistence that her children must not know the details of what he had done on her orders.

Among the items tucked in around her were Albert's dressing gown, a lock of her favourite servant John Brown's hair (concealed with flowers in order to avoid upsetting Victoria's children, who had disapproved of the pair's closeness) and a ring that had belonged to Brown's own mother.

Victoria's beloved Indian Munshi ('clerk' or 'teacher'), Abdul Karim, was banished from court soon after Edward VII took the throne. Karim's close relationship with the late queen after the loss of John Brown had been another source of unease amongst her children and courtiers. No time was wasted in moving him safely away from the British monarchy, to the estate that Victoria had bestowed upon him in the city of Agra, in the north Indian state of Upper Pradesh.

Society as a whole had increasingly pushed the boundaries of both sexual and social freedom during the 1800s, but, by the end of Victoria's reign, it had been squashed back down to a point where it looked at least as though the Establishment was back in control. The new king would bring some of his previous misbehaviour to the throne with him, but the general public felt that he did at least have a sense of humour and there was perhaps more hope in the world. Little did they realise the horrors of war that loomed little more than a decade ahead.

There was plenty to be positive about. Improvements in the manufacturing process meant that condoms were now far easier to get hold of and to use (although ironically, the majority were imported from Germany). This didn't immediately translate into lower rates of disease, mostly because of the stigma that was still attached to their use, but they did eventually become accepted and used more widely.

Childbirth was becoming safer and less painful, thanks to the increasing acceptance of chloroform and morphine over the previous few decades (helped on its way enormously by Victoria's use of chloroform during the birth of Prince Leopold way back in 1853). It was still far from an exact science, and any such intervention faced opposition from those who believed that pain was the woman's punishment for 'original sin' (while handily managing to avoid punishing the father), but women had realised that it was possible to numb at least some of the horrors of childbirth and many were determined to take advantage of anything that might help.

It would be 1937 before the next Matrimonial Causes Act made the divorce courts more of a level playing field between men and women, but rumblings were already being heard, with a Royal Commission recommending some liberalisation of the laws as early as 1912.

The Criminal Law Amendment Act did indeed help to safeguard the welfare of many women and girls, as well as effectively making childhood last longer due to the raising of the age of consent. However, the criminalisation of homosexuality was to hang like a shadow over the country for almost another century. Oscar Wilde had died less than two months before Victoria, with something of the sexual rebellion dying with him.

Women's progress towards equality marched on apace and the country would soon be agog at the violence meted out both by and towards the suffragettes. Victorian progress in transport – bicycles and the rail network, as well as the omnibus service and the new London Underground – gave women increasing freedom by default. It's very difficult to supervise someone's behaviour if they're mobile.

The killer cholera epidemics of the nineteenth century led to John Snow discovering the link between bacterium and tainted water supplies, which in turn was the impetus for Joseph Bazalgette's great works in developing the London sewage and drainage system. Late Victorian liberalism sowed the seed for the welfare state, although it would be a long time coming.

The Britain that Victoria left to the son she disliked so much was very different to the one she had taken control of more than six decades earlier. Her reign marked the beginnings of the truly modern age.

> "'Tut, tut, child!" said the Duchess. "Everything's got a moral, if only you can find it."'
>
> The Mock Turtle's Story, *Alice in Wonderland.*

Index

abortion; 20-22
abstinence; 65
adoption; 23-24
Albert Edward, Prince of Wales;
    33-34, 48-50
Albert of Saxe-Coburg and Gotha,
    Prince Consort; 48
Albert Victor, Prince, Duke of
    Clarence and Avondale; 91
Alexandra of Denmark,
    Princess; 50
Alice's Adventures in Wonderland,
    book by Lewis Carroll; 111,
    112, 115
An Gorta Mór - see Great Famine
Anatomical Venus; 44
Anthony, Susan B.; 16
Armstrong, Eliza; 70-72
Arthur, Lord Somerset; 91
Arthur's Flogging, story
    by Algernon Charles
    Swinburne; 48
Ashbee, Henry Spencer; 53-54
Awakening Conscience, The,
    painting by William Holman
    Hunt; 102-103

Baartman, Sarah 4
baby farming; 23-24
Baker-Brown, Isaac; 43-44
Balcombe, Florence; 108

basiotribe; 64
Bathory, Elizabeth; 110
Bazalgette, Joseph; 115
Bell, Laura; 81-83
Bertie, *see* 'Albert Edward, Prince
    of Wales'
Besant, Annie; 65
bibi, denoting a mistress; 36-37
Bicycle Face, supposed disease of
    female cyclists; 15'
Blandford, George; 26
Blue Funnel Line, the; 37-38
Bookseller's Row; 52
Booth, Bramwell; 71
Boulton, Thomas Ernest; 87-89
Bradlaugh; Charles; 65
Bradley, Katherine; 93
breach of promise; 20
Britain, population of; *xiii*
Brontë, Charlotte; 101
Brown, Ford Maddox; 104
Brown, John; 113
Brownlow Hill workhouse; 75
Buggery Act 1533, the; 91-92
Butler, Josephine; 73-76; charitable
    work, 74-75; LNA, association
    with, 76

caesarian section; 64
calling cards, 6
Carlyle, Jane; 31-32

Carlyle, Thomas; 31-32

Carmilla, novel by Sheridan Le Fanu; 109-110

Carroll, Lewis *see* Dodgson, Charles Lutwidge

Chaplin, Rt Hon Henry, 1st Viscount Chaplin; 7-8

Chapman, Annie; 77

Charles II, King; 67

childbed fever; 63

childbirth; 63-64, 114

chloroform; 114

cholera; 114

Cleveland Street Scandal, the; 90-91

Clifden, Nellie; 49

Clinton, Stella *see* Boulton, Thomas Ernest

clitoridectomy; 43-44

Coal Hole, The; 51

Cole, Viscount Lowery; 33

Coleridge-Taylor, Samuel; 38

Collier, John; 103

Combe, George; 49

combinations; 13

condoms; 66-67, 114

Conroy, Sir John; *x-xi*

consent, age of; *xiv*

Contagious Diseases Act(s); 73-74, 75-76

contraception; 20, 65-67

Cooper, Edith; 93

corsets; 10, 11

Criminal Law Amendment Act 1885; 71, 91, 94, 95, 97, 98, 99

crinolines; 10

Cullwick, Hannah; 45-48

cycling; 15-16

debutantes; 6-7

diachylon; 21-22

dildo; 41-42

divorce; 34-36

Dodgson, Charles Lutwidge; 111-112

Douglas, Alfred 'Bosie'; 97, 99

Douglas, Francis Archibald, Viscount Drumlarig; 97-98

Douglas, John Sholto, Marquess of Queensberry; 26-27, 97-98

Dracula, novel by Bram Stoker; 106-107, 108, 109, 110

Drumaconnor House; 12

Drysdale, George; 42-43

Dugdale, William; 52-53, 96

Dyer, Amelia; 24

Eagle, Georgiana; 5

East Lynne, novel by Ellen Wood; 101-102

Eddowes, Catherine; 77

Education and Employment of Women, The by Josephine Butler; 75

Ellis, Agnes; 68

Empire, British; 36-37

Field, Michael; 92-93

flagellation; 48

foetal destruction; 64

foundling hospitals; 24-25

freak shows; 4

Fruits of Philosophy, by Charles Knowlton; 65-66

General Paralysis of the Insane (GPI); 60, 61

Gladstone, Catherine; 81

Gladstone, William Ewart, politician and Prime Minister; 43, 80-81, 83

gonorrhoea; 62, 73

Gordon, Alexander; 63

Great Famine, the; 37
Greville, Daisy, Countess of
    Warwick, 9
Gropecunt Lane, Shrewsbury; 85
gross indecency; 97

Hammond, Charles; 90
Harker, Mina; 106, 107
Hastings, Marquess of; 7-8
Hawarden Castle; 80, 81
Hayden, Maria B.; 5
Highgate; 68, 69; cemetery; 68-70,
    101, 104-105
Hodson, Henrietta; 95
Hoffs, Gill; 11-12
Holman Hunt, William; 102-103
Holywell Street; 51-52, 56, 58, 96
Hottentot Venus, the 4
Howell, Charles Augustus; 105
hysteria; 39-40, 44

India; 36-37
infant mortality; 62-63
infanticide; 22-24
Irving, Henry; 108-109
Ivanhoe, book by Sir Walter Scott; 2

Jane Eyre, novel by Charlotte
    Brontë; 101
Jarrett, Rebecca; 70, 71-72
Jewsbury, Geraldine; 31
Johnstone, Sir Frederick; 33
Jones, Emma; 69-70

Karim, Abdul; 113
Kelly, Mary Jane; 77
Kensington System; x-xi
Keppel, Alice; 50
King Edward, *see* 'Albert Edward'
Kings Head, public house in
    Shrewsbury; 84

Kipling, Rudyard, *On The City
    Wall*; 72
Knowlton, Charles; 65-66

Labouchère, Henry; 80, 94-97, 99
labour dystocia; 64
Lack, Esther; 23
Ladies National Association
    (LNA); 76
Lambert, E. & Sons, Dalston; 67
Lanchester, Edith 'Biddy'; 25-27
Lanchester, Elsa; 27
Lane, Edward; 35-36
Langtry, Lillie; 8, 9, 50
Lazenby, William; 41, 54
Le Fanu, Joseph Thomas Sheridan;
    109-110
lesbianism; 93-94
lifespan, expected; *xiv*
Lilith, painting by John Collier; 103
Linton, Eliza Lynn; 17-18
Lister, Joseph; 63
Liverpool 37-38; docks 37-38;
    prostitution 71-72, 76-77;
    Chinatown 38
lock hospital; 74
Lockwood, Frank, QC; 98
London Diocesan Penitentiary;
    68, 69
love chair; 49

Magdalene asylums / laundries;
    27-28
Maggie Mae, Liverpool folk song;
    72-73
*Maiden Tribute of Modern Babylon,
    the*, newspaper scandal; 71
Malicious Shooting and Stabbing
    Act 1803; 21
Mardol, Shrewsbury; 84
Marmon, Doris; 24

Marmon, Evelina; 23-24
Married Women's Property Act
    1882; 30
Marryat, Captain Frederick; 3-4
masturbation; 42, 43, 44, 45
Matrimonial Causes Act
    1937; 114
mercury (in medical treatment); 59,
    60, 62
Millais, Sir John Everett;
    103-104
Miller, James; 77
Moncrieffe, Harriet; 33-34
Mordaunt, Lady Harriet; *see*
    Moncrieffe, Harriet
Mordaunt, Sir Charles; 33-34
Munby, Arthur; 45-48
Munby, Hannah - *see* Cullwick,
    Hannah
Mundell, Hugh Alexander; 87-88
My Secret Life, book by 'Walter';
    53-54

Nicholls, Mary Anne; 77, 79

Obscene Publications Act 1857; 52
Offences Against the Person Act;
    1875, *xiv;* 1861, 92
orgasm, female: 30, 31

Paget, Lady Florence; 7-8
Pall Mall Gazette, The; 70-71
Park, Fanny Winifred *see* Park,
    Frederick William
Park, Frederick William;
    87-89
Parker-Bowles, Camilla; 50
Paul, Dr James; 88
Pearl, The, pornographic magazine;
    42, 57
Pepper's Ghost, illusion trick; 5

Photography, erotic; 56-57
picker (occupation); 13
Poe, Edgar Allen; 44
Polidori, John; 106
Pomeroy, Florence, Viscountess
    Harberton; 17
Poor Law Act 1834; 20
Pratt, James; 92
Pre-Raphaelite Brotherhood, the;
    102, 103, 105
pregnancy; 62-65
Primrose, Archibald, Earl of
    Rosebery; 98
Priory Hospital, the; 26-27
prostitution; 61-62, 69, 73-86
Psycho Ladies Cycle; 16
puerperal fever; 63
puerperal insanity; 23
Pulsocon, Dr Macaura's; 40

Queensberry, Marquess of *see*
    Douglas, John Sholto

Raj, British; 36-37
Rana, Jung Bahadur, Nepalese
    Prime Minister, 82
Rational Dress Society, The;
    16-17
Rectorotor; 41
Regina vs Wilde, court case; 97-99
rickets; 64
Ripper, serial killer; 77-80
Robinson, Henry Oliver; 35-36
Robinson, Isabella; 35-36
Romanticism; 1
Rossetti, Christina; 102
Rossetti, Dante Gabriel;
    102, 104-105
Rotten Row; 14
Roushill, Shrewsbury; 84, 85
Rubenhold, Hallie; 78, 79

sailor's 'wives'; 25
Salop Penitentiary; 85-86
Salvation Army; 71
Saul, Jack; 54-55
Scott, Sir Walter; 2
seances, 4-5
Semmelweiz, Ignaz; 64
Sexual Offences Act 1967; 99
Shadwell, Arthur; 15-16
Sheffield, lead poisonings and
    miscarriage; 21
Shelley, Mary; 100
Shrewsbury; 84-86
Shwabe, Maurice; 98-99
Siddal, Elizabeth 'Lizzie'; 102,
    103-105
sidesaddle, style of horse riding; 14
Sins of the Cities of the Plain, The,
    book by 'Jack Saul'; 55
Sisters of Our Lady of Charity
    (Irish convent); 27-28
Smith, John; 92
Society for the Suppression of
    Vice; 52
Spencer-Churchill, Jennie; 50
spermatorrhoea; 44, 45
spiritualism; 5
Starley Bros, bicycle
    manufacturers; 16
Stead, William Thomas; 70-72, 95,
    96-97
Stoker, Bram; 106-109, 110, 111
Stopes, Charlotte; 17
Stride, Elizabeth; 77
Sturm und Drang; 2
Sullivan, Shamus 'James'; 26-27
Summerscale, Kate, *Mrs
    Robinson's Disgrace*; 35
Swinburne, Algernon Charles; 48
Swinscow, Charles; 90
syphilis; 59-61, 73

tableau vivant; 51
telegraph boys; 90-91
Temperance Hall raid, Hulme; 89-90
Thistlethwayte, Captain Augustus;
    82-83
Thistlethwayte, Laura *see* Bell,
    Laura

Van Helsing, Abraham; 106,
    107, 109
vibrator; 39-40
Victoria, Princess of Saxe-Coburg-
    Saalfeld, Duchess of Kent, *x-xi*
Victoria, Queen; childhood *x - xi*;
    coronation *x*; marriage 2-3, 31;
    views on lesbianism, 93-94;
    death, 113
Victorian Gothic (in literature);
    105-106
Vinegar Valentines; 8
virginity, female; 19-20, male; 29

Walmisley, Jessie; 38
Walter (author); 53-54
Westenra, Lucy; 106-107,
Whippingham Papers, The,
    erotica; 48
Whitechapel murders; 77-80
Whitman, Walt; 108, 109
Wilde, Constance; 17
Wilde, Emily; 12
Wilde, Jane; 108
Wilde, Mary; 12
Wilde, Oscar; half sisters 12; trial,
    97-99; friendship with Bram
    Stoker, 108, 109; Paris 99;
    death, 110-111
Wilde, William; 12, 81
Wood, Ellen; 101-102

Yokel's Preceptor, The; 96